Pelican Books
Economics of the Real World

Peter Donaldson was born in Manchester in 1934 but
left shortly afterwards for Kent, where he went to
Gillingham Grammar School and won an open
scholarship to Balliol. He read politics, philosophy
and economics, and graduated from Oxford in 1956.
He then taught very briefly in a secondary modern
school and for two years in a college of technology
before taking up a university appointment at Leeds.
He was a lecturer in the department of economics at
Leicester University 1959–62, when he also did a
good deal of work for the Leicester and Nottingham
University adult education departments and for the
Workers' Educational Association.

At the end of 1962, he was one of the first British
university teachers to be seconded to key positions in
underdeveloped countries under the scheme for
Commonwealth Educational Cooperation. He was
appointed, for two years, as Visiting Reader in
Economics at the Osmania University, Hyderabad,
and subsequently extended his stay in India to four
years.

Since 1967 he has been Tutor in Economics at
Ruskin College, Oxford. In recent years he has done a
considerable amount of broadcasting, including two
series for radio, *Managing the Economy* and
Affluence and Inequality – and two for B.B.C.
television, *Economics of the Real World* and *Peter
Donaldson's Illustrated Economics*. His publications
include *Worlds Apart*, *Economics of the Real World*,
Peter Donaldson's Illustrated Economics and *Guide
to the British Economy*. Many of his books have been
published in Pelicans.

He is married and has three children.

Peter Donaldson

Economics of the
Real World

British Broadcasting Corporation
and Penguin Books

Published by the British Broadcasting Corporation
35 Marylebone High Street, London WIM 4AA

ISBN 0 563 10777 4

and by

Penguin Books Ltd, Harmondsworth, Middlesex, England
Penguin Books, 625 Madison Avenue,
New York, New York 10022, U.S.A.
Penguin Books Australia Ltd, Ringwood, Victoria, Australia
Penguin Books Canada Ltd,
2801 John Street, Markham, Ontario, Canada L3R 1B4
Penguin Books (N.Z.) Ltd, 182–190 Wairau Road,
Auckland 10, New Zealand

ISBN 02 1775 4

Published in Pelican Books 1973
Reprinted 1973, 1974, 1975, 1976 (twice), 1977

Copyright © Peter Donaldson, 1973
All rights reserved

Made and printed in Great Britain by
Hazell Watson & Viney Ltd, Aylesbury, Bucks
Set in Linotype Plantin

Contents

Preface

The paternity of *Economics of the Real World* changed while it was in an embryonic form. Initially sired by Penguins, it became a joint publication with the B.B.C. as a result of my subsequent involvement with the television series of the same title. This meant some modification of the original conception: it seemed sensible to give it a structure which fitted in with the twenty-part television programme format, and rather more basic exposition was called for. However, although I hope the book will be useful for those who watch the series, it is still primarily intended to have an existence independent of it.

It is written for those non-economists and introductory students of economics who may have been put off by various aspects of the subject: its jargon and mystique, its unreality and lack of concern with people and their problems. The aim is to give the reader a simple account of some of the main elements of economics, to draw together various strands of criticisms of both economics and economic policy, and to try to bring out into the open the underlying values of our economic system which everyone is qualified to discuss – matters like the old-fashioned but still unresolved issues of inequality and unfairness with which much of the book is concerned.

My thanks are due to a number of people. Peter Wright, chief editor of Penguins, in his loyalty and dedication is an author's ideal publisher. Bernard Adams and Chris Jelley, my producers for the television series, were immensely helpful – both in their 'nitpicking' at a draft stage and in bringing to bear a general perspective. Their curiosity about the content of the later chapters while I was still wrestling with the early ones seemed at the time premature (although necessary for their programme planning); in fact, of course, it was invaluable to have been forced to think out the overall structure at that early stage. To Robert Albury, also of the B.B.C., I am very grateful for research and preparation of tables and figures which he masterfully accomplished with his usual languid efficiency.

I am indebted to all those, mentioned in the text or not, whose work I have as usual shamelessly drawn upon. Also to Sandra Wilson who typed the final manuscript with almost alarming speed and competence.

Finally, an apology. For the second year running I have imposed on my family the absences, irritations and general gloom involved in writing to a demanding deadline. Even the dog has suffered. To Sheila and Sally, Adam and Amanda – my love, thanks and a promise that it won't happen again. At least for a while.

I

Economists and the Economy

Economics isn't very easy to get on with. Nor, for the most part, are its practitioners. Most people are still rather nervous of economists. They view them with an uneasy mixture of awe at their authority and a growing suspicion that in fact economists may not be very good at dealing with the real problems which face us.

But for the non-economist it is difficult to be sure. While general elections are won and lost on what are ostensibly economic issues, the ordinary voter has to make up his mind in almost total economic darkness. He may hold emphatic views, but they are generally based on economic folklore – a bundle of misconceptions, fallacies and superstition. Even the well-informed, prepared to air their knowledgeable opinions on most other topics under the sun, will cheerfully confess ignorance when it comes to economics.

Such widespread economic illiteracy is really rather serious. Today a modicum of economic knowledge is a vital part of political education. But surprisingly little effort has been made to impart any understanding of economic issues to the general public. At schools and colleges economics is for the specialists. The mass media tend to discuss such matters at a level of comfortable superficiality. And economists themselves have shown little interest in sharing their secrets with outsiders. They have generally preferred to maintain the mystique of their discipline by talking in a mandarin jargon which only the initiated can hope to understand. Indeed, so uncommunicative are economists as a breed that they have the greatest difficulty in talking to each other.

Economics under Fire

Lacking the technical armoury with which to stand up to the economists on their own ground, laymen can only voice vague doubts about what it is that economists are up to. But in recent years the doubts have become stronger. More and more people *are* asking why, when there is greater economic expertise in government than ever before, does the economy still fail to work as we want it to. Students, perhaps lacking the mature sophistication to see the Emperor's clothes, sometimes ungratefully challenge the economic gospel with the gibe that it is nothing more than a defence of a bourgeois dreamworld. But most impressive of all is the increasing rumble of self-questioning from within the economic establishment itself.

For Joan Robinson, for example, Professor of Economics at Cambridge, the writing on the wall is very clear indeed. In December 1971 she warned her fellow-economists: 'The cranks and critics flourish because orthodox economists have neglected the great problems which everyone else feels to be urgent and menacing.' Arguing that economics was now in a state of acute crisis, she pointed to a particularly disturbing area of economists' neglect – the fundamental question of income distribution. Her conclusion was: 'We have nothing to say on the subject which above all others occupies the minds of people whom economics is supposed to enlighten.'[1]

In a 1972 edition of the *Economic Journal*, the official organ of the Royal Economic Society, *two* articles by eminent economists were devoted to criticizing the present state of economics and its lack of recent progress. Professor Phelps Brown, of London University, entitled his Presidential Address to the Society 'The Underdevelopment of Economics', and took as his starting point 'the smallness of the contribution that the most conspicuous developments of economics in the last quarter of a century have made to the most pressing problems of our times'. G. D. N. Worswick, Director of the National Institute of Economic and Social Research, asking 'Is Progress in Economic Science

1. J. Robinson, 'The Second Crisis of Economic Theory', *American Economics Association Papers and Proceedings*, May 1972, p. 8.

Possible?', also expressed his uneasiness. 'The standards are high, the intellectual battalions are powerful, but notwithstanding the appearance of formidable progress in techniques of all kinds the performance of economics seems curiously disappointing, the moment one puts a few test questions.' The first of Mr Worswick's test questions was simply – what are the causes of inflation in the United Kingdom at the present time?

The charge against economists is, above all, that of irrelevance. Economics, to the outsider, might seem an inherently earthy study rooted firmly in the worldly stuff of everyday life. But the world about which economists have commonly woven their theories has generally been one of their own making, remote from reality itself. There are two main reasons for this.

The first stems from the technical immaturity of the subject. The study of economics is still a relatively new one. Although quite a lot of progress has been made in understanding how the economy works, the areas of economic ignorance – questions to which economists should honestly answer 'We simply don't know' – are far more widespread than the general public (and sometimes governments) usually think. There are too few economists prepared to agree with Professor Phelps Brown that 'our own science has hardly reached its seventeenth century'.[2]

Faced with the problem of explaining a complex reality, the economist's approach is to reduce that reality to a simplified 'model' which can be more easily handled. In itself, such a method is perfectly proper. But in economics it has often had disastrous consequences. Having built up a model in the first place, economists have proved very reluctant ever to modify or replace it. The result is that what may once have been a rough representation of the real world becomes, after a time, nothing but a theoretical abstraction; its abstruseness in the face of major structural and institutional changes is increasingly evident to students of the subject. Worse still is the way in which economists, having deduced how things would work in the pretend-world of their own models, then treat their theories as proven economic truths and suggest that they can be applied wholesale

2. E. H. Phelps Brown, 'The Underdevelopment of Economics', *Economic Journal*, March 1972, p. 10.

in the real world of economic policy. They have often been wrong. 'The consistently indifferent performance in practical application is in fact a symptom of the fundamental imbalance of our discipline. The weak and all too slowly growing empirical foundation clearly cannot support the proliferating superstructure of pure, or should I say speculative, economic theory.'[3]

Apart from its technical immaturity, there is a more profound reason why economics is accused of being remote from the real world. Many economists claim to be scientists just as much as physicists or chemists are, though they have a special handicap in being unable to perform laboratory experiments. Now adherence to scientific principles is a very good thing if it means simply that economists recognize that they must submit their hypotheses to rigorous testing before they elevate them to the status of accepted knowledge. In fact, however, this discipline of scientific method is not something which economists have shown much interest in; on the contrary, nearly every introductory economics text is brimful of untested hypotheses passing as received economic theory. No, it is a quite different aspect of the scientific imprimatur which principally appeals to economists. As scientists, they claim to study what *is* rather than what *ought* to be. They can make statements with *objective* authority – as distinct from the value-ridden propositions of politicians and the rest. Theirs are purely technical conclusions derived from detached, impartial analysis, only at a later stage sullied and muddied by the value judgements of those who are responsible for acting upon them or who feel their consequences.

In fact, economics is far from value-free. Bias appears both in selection of the questions deemed to be legitimate subjects of economic analysis and in the ways in which those questions are treated. Issues of economic justice, for example, are considered non-scientific, while at the same time something like 'free competition' can be analysed with an apparent impartiality which conceals the fact, as Myrdal puts it, that proof of its theoretical effectiveness transforms it into a 'political desideratum'.

Economics claims to be value-free and is nothing of the sort.

3. W. Leontief, 'Theoretical Assumptions and Non-observed Facts', *American Economic Review*, 1971, p. 1.

But its pseudo-scientific pretensions set it apart from the real world of emotions, values and prejudices from which it tries to remain aloof. Economics and economic policy cannot be devoid of values if they are to be taken·as serious attempts to cope with the problems of the world in which we live. The matters which concern people – questions of where they stand in relation to others, the nature of their working conditions, the quality of life in its many aspects – these are the real issues which economics can neglect only at peril of becoming totally irrelevant. To be of any help, economists *have* to begin from a set of values and be prepared to use their analysis instrumentally, in revealing, not just how the economy works now, but also how it ought to work. Economists are not, however, philosopher-kings. They have no *special* right to dictate how society should behave and be governed. But they have as much right as·anyone else. And if they are to be concerned with issues most relevant to the real world, then the value-content of economics must be declared rather than denied.

Why Economists Disagree

To outsiders, one of the main factors undermining the credibility of economists is their notorious inability to agree about anything at all. But, given the nature and limitations of economics which we have just been discussing, the failure of economists to speak with a single voice is easily explicable. Only *if* economics were the mature, objective science which it pretends to be – only *if* it consisted of a body of proven, value-free theories – could we expect different economists always to come to similar conclusions. Since it is not that at all, the lack of agreement among economists is inevitable.

Take, for example, the question of whether Britain should have joined Europe. During the course of the 'Great Debate', Professor Kaldor of Cambridge University organized a letter to *The Times* opposing British entry. The letter was signed by no less than 153 academic and business economists. A few days later, another letter was published in *The Times* supporting British membership of the E.E.C. and signed by 141 professional economists.

How could this come about? How could the profession be split down the middle on an issue about which non-economists might reasonably expect clear guidance from the experts?

Partly it was the result of sheer technical ignorance. Economics could provide no clear-cut answers to the questions of what the *static* advantages and disadvantages of British entry would be – the effects of increased specialization and trade between members of an enlarged Community – or what the *dynamic* effects would be of increased scale of production, greater mobility of labour and capital, and joining a bloc with a record of faster economic growth than Britain. Even the direction of the changes which would follow British entry was unknown, let alone when their impact would be felt or how great it would be. Economists simply didn't know. But that unfortunately did not deter them from making firm, albeit widely different, predictions.

Beyond that, the great divide in economic opinion stemmed from the quite different value premisses on which the two groups based their analysis. Thus some supported British entry because they saw in a wider Europe a strengthening of western capitalism against economic and political threats from both within and without. Others opposed it on precisely the same grounds. But this was no simple split between 'left-wing' and 'right-wing' economists. Because nobody knew what the consequences would be (although they often *thought* that they did), it was equally possible for both left and right to come to the same conclusion that Britain *should* join Europe – or for them both to parade under the Anti-Market banner.

It may seem somewhat perverse to introduce a subject by harping on its inadequacies. But if Leontief is right in saying that 'Economics today rides the crest of intellectual respectability and popular acclaim' and that 'The serious attention with which our pronouncements are received by the general public, hard-bitten politicians, and even sceptical businessmen is second only to that which was given to physicists and space experts a few years ago when the round trip to the moon seemed to be our only truly national goal'.[4] then it is important that we should be fully aware of the limitations of economics. Economists cannot

4. Leontief, op. cit.

always be relied upon to remind us of them, although, as we have seen, there are some who are acutely aware that their discipline is in a state of crisis.

Nonetheless in recent decades governments have increasingly acted on economic advice. To prove the pudding, to see the strength of economics as well as its weaknesses, we must look at the performance of the economy over this period.

The Economic Record

An extraordinary number of people in this country seem to think that during the course of their lifetimes the state of the economy has gone from bad to worse. They may disagree about the time pattern of the great economic slide. Some would argue that it has been a gradual deterioration over a long period. Others, of both political colours, detect an acceleration in the rate of decline – pointing to nothing less than imminent economic collapse. The breakdown of liberal civilization? The final death-throes of capitalism? Where will it all end? Things can't go on as they are ...

The British have a probably unparalleled capacity for what has been called 'economasochism'. In this country, we are quite obsessed by the state of the economy – its current crisis vying with the weather as a topic of conversation. And who can blame us? For our sense of foreboding is the product of years of listening to, watching and reading the doom-laden predictions of politicians and observers warning of one economic disaster after another. We *know* that we are suffering from some deep-seated malaise because we have been told it so often. Here is just one typically depressing summary of the situation:

Sixty years ago England had leadership in most branches of industry. It was inevitable that she should cede much of that leadership. It was not inevitable that she should lose so much of it as she has done . . . England is like a composite photograph, in which two likenesses are blurred into one. It shows traces of American enterprise and German order, but the enterprise is faded and the order muddled. They combine to a curious travesty in which activity and perseverance assume the expression of ease and indolence. The once enterprising manufacturer has grown slack, he has let the business take care of itself, while he is shooting grouse or yachting in the

Mediterranean. That is *his* business. The once unequalled workman has adopted the motto 'get as much and do as little as possible'. Each blames the other.

A pungent, if slightly florid, résumé of the British economic decline and its causes. What is interesting is that the quotation is from Arthur Shadwell's *Industrial Efficiency* – published in 1909. And those convinced that the main source of Britain's economic ills is on the shop floor may also relish Shadwell's quotation from a contemporary German observer:

> Your workers are determined to level down, not to level up. The majority read little but the sporting press, and care for little but betting and sport. It is always a source of wonder to me, after seeing, as I have seen, the thousands who go to Lords or the Oval on some week-day, not a holiday – and you live now in almost perpetual holiday – that any work at all is done in England. If your men idle two or three days in the week, and do less than they ought to do on the other four, they cannot wonder that they don't hold their own or that there are many unemployed.

The Times in 1901 and 1902 published a series of articles on 'The Crisis of British Industry' which also saw as the villain of the piece the practices of the trade unions – in opposing mechanization, in restricting output and in maintaining archaic apprenticeship rules.

But in the decades around the turn of the century a first airing was being given to a variety of other explanations of our alleged economic backwardness compared with the United States and Germany. Some laid the blame at the door of managerial conservatism. For example, American industrialists were more readily prepared to replace obsolete equipment 'due to a psychological difference between the adventurous employer of the United States and the more conservative British employers'.[5] Others emphasized the problem of recruiting management and its dilettantism: '[The] best brains of our upper classes will go anywhere but into industry – into a bank or a merchant's office perhaps, but not into horny-handed manufacture.'[6] 'There still

5. Quoted in A. L. Levine, *Industrial Retardation in Britain 1880–1914*, Weidenfeld & Nicolson, 1967, p. 69.
6. ibid., p. 73.

exists . . . a strong preference for the man trained from an early age in the works, and a prejudice against the so-called "college-trained" man.'[7] Or was the root of the problem neglect of technical education or lack of interest in technology generally? 'It is rather in the greater application of science to industry where we have fallen short.'[8]

The idea that there is something fundamentally amiss with the British economy is clearly not a new one – and neither are the current explanations. And yet somehow we have survived. Could it be that for all these years we have been grappling with non-problems, that our fears of economic insanity were illusory? To some extent this is so. There *are* things profoundly wrong with the way in which the economy has worked, and continues to work. That indeed is the argument of much of this book. But these deficiencies are not appropriately measured by the usual indicators – of employment, economic growth, balance of payments statistics and price indices. Looking at *those*, the economic record is in fact a great deal more favourable than is popularly supposed.

So, to keep matters in perspective, let us look in the first place at the credit side of the economic balance sheet and see how, in many ways, British economic performance must be judged remarkably successful – how, on several counts, the economy can be said to be running better now than ever before. Comparing, for example, the seventies and the thirties, there are a number of major 'successes' to record.

The most obvious of these concerns employment. In this respect, the 1930s represented one of the most tragically absurd episodes in our economic history. While economists continued to define their study as one which essentially dealt with problems arising from the *scarcity* of resources in relation to apparently unlimited demands upon them, the facts of the matter were very different. Far from being scarce – with fierce competition for their use – a large proportion of resources in advanced industrial nations at that time were actually lying idle, with no one interested in using them. While machines rusted in empty factories, while firms faced bankruptcy, their potential customers,

7. ibid., p. 75.   8. ibid, p. 69.

the workers, stood by their millions in dole queues or filed past in hunger marches.

There was nothing very novel about this. Periodic bouts of unemployment had characterized capitalist economies since the onset of industrialization. The gap between the problems which engaged economists and the facts of the real world had been present for a long time. All that was new about the thirties was that the divergence had never before been so acute and plain to see. What distinguished the unemployment of the thirties from what had gone before was simply its enormity. During the inter-war years unemployment *averaged* no less than 14 per cent.

The record since the war has been very dramatically better. For most of the period, unemployment has been between 1 and 2 per cent of the work-force – an almost incredible contrast with the pre-war situation. Admittedly, during the late sixties and early seventies there was a deterioration; at times, nearly a million people in Britain were without jobs. But even that represents well under 4 per cent of the work-force. Anything approaching that figure is highly unsatisfactory, but recent unemployment is nonetheless in a quite different league from that of the thirties.

Equally contrasting is the performance of the economy with regard to economic growth. The thirties were the heyday of a group of economists known as the 'stagnationists', who gloomily predicted that the era of economic expansion was over. They argued that the great growth impulses of the nineteenth century had now spent themselves and that 'mature' economies such as those of the United States and Western Europe were doomed to secular stagnation. No longer could population growth be relied upon to stimulate further industrial investment (indeed, in the thirties, books were being written on the implications of a declining population); there were no great new markets to be opened as in the nineteenth century; the industrial revolution was over and technological progress could no longer provide its earlier impetus.

All these predictions have proved wrong in the post-war period. Far from being stagnant, advanced western economies since the war have grown very rapidly, often at historically unprecedented rates. In Britain, where we are much prone to lament our inadequacies in this respect, the economy has managed to expand its output of goods and services in post-war years by an average of some 2½ per cent per annum. This figure is generally referred to disparagingly as 'only' 2½ per cent. Yet it is a rate of growth higher than Britain ever sustained in the past – including the industrial revolution, when it had a head start over other countries. So, once again, the economic record must be marked 'fairly good' when judged by historical standards.

The post-war international performance of the economy, on the other hand, hardly looks like a success story. The balance of payments has been a perpetual worry, with crisis following crisis with monotonous regularity. Massive international debts, persistent loss of confidence by foreigners and a pound devalued on three occasions – these are the common attributes of an economy trying to live beyond its means. But this is very misleading, and in many ways our international position has substantially improved since the 1930s. For example, before the war no less than one third of our imports were paid for, not by exports, but by earnings on past overseas investments. During recent years, this 'trade gap' has become of very much more manageable proportions, and the restructuring of the economy which has made this possible is no mean achievement. Then again, balance of payments deficits have been *relatively* insignificant: a deficit of £500 million, for instance, sounds far less alarming when it is remembered that it is little more than 1 per cent of our gross national output – less than the amount by which we have managed on average to *increase* national output each year. And finally, although Britain does have large international debts, the amount which foreigners owe us is much larger; Britain continues to be a major international creditor. Certainly, there *are* problems on the international front, but they hardly threaten national solvency.

But what about prices? The economy has suffered from persistent inflation throughout the post-war period. This, however, is not just a post-war phenomenon: prices have risen every year since 1934. Nor has there been any cumulative worsening of inflation over the period as a whole, although in recent years price increases have been at particularly worrying levels. But the problem is not a peculiarly British one. Other economies have faced the same problem. Some have done better at containing inflation, but many have managed markedly worse than the United Kingdom. Moreover, although the *cost* of living has regularly increased, so also has the *standard* of living of the majority of British people. Incomes and output have risen faster than prices, so that we are substantially better off in real terms – whether it seems like it or not.

It can be argued, then, that the economy today – at least when judged by conventional criteria – is working better than it ever has. But that is not to say that all is lovely in the economic garden. In the first place, none of the economic objectives of post-war governments has been fully achieved. We have not managed to run the economy at consistently full employment; in particular, regional disparities in employment continue to be a matter of serious concern. Our record on economic growth has been a far cry from the targets which successive governments have set themselves and from what other countries have managed to achieve. The balance of payments has continued to be a policy headache. And no one can be satisfied with the recent record on prices. We have not done badly, but why have we not managed to do much better? Why have the conventional economic objectives been so difficult to achieve? Are there basic incompatibilities which prevent us having simultaneously full employment, rapid economic growth, and price and balance of payments stability? Are we in fact condemned to the life of stop–go which has dominated the economy throughout the post-war period?

Then again, if the performance of the economy has been good when compared with earlier periods, how far is this due to increased economic understanding? To what extent should the credit go to economists – or would the economy have fared as well even if governments had never heeded a word of economic advice?

The technical problems of managing the economy to achieve conventional economic objectives and how far economists have been able to help in overcoming them – these form the subject matter of coming chapters. It will involve a brief excursion into some basic economic theory (Chapters 2–4) followed by a critical look at economic policy-making in post-war Britain (Chapters 5–8).

But when that is done, far more significant questions will remain unanswered. The subsequent argument will be that the so-called 'ends' of economic policy – full employment, rapid economic growth, balance of payments equilibrium and price stability – are nothing of the sort. They are means rather than ends – and it is ends which concern ordinary people. What makes economics seem unreal and remote from them is the fact that it never seems directed towards matters which are of urgent importance in their everyday lives. Thus people are not generally interested in overall 'full employment', but in the question of jobs for whom, where, and doing what in what conditions. The 'rate of economic growth' is of no real concern to you or me; what matters is what is happening to our standard of living, what an increase in national output is made up of, and the cost to ourselves and our environment of achieving it. Above all, perhaps, we are concerned with the issue of equity – whether or not the economic system is working *fairly*. The distribution of income and wealth, how much we get and have compared with others, occupies a central place in most people's thoughts about economics.

This is the stuff of the real world. It is a world apart from that of employment statistics, exchange rates, stock-market valuations and the gross national product. The real world is often incapable of precise measurement; it is not a clinical laboratory in which economic experiments can be carefully conducted. It is a world of which prejudices and values are an inextricable part rather than a veneer which must be delicately removed and set aside before objective analysis can begin. For that reason it is a world which economics has largely neglected.

2

Before and after Keynes

One of the classic definitions of economics was given by Professor Lionel Robbins in *The Nature and Significance of Economic Science* (1934), where he describes it as: 'The Science which studies human behaviour as a relationship between ends and scarce means which have alternative uses.' This definition, though in some ways unsatisfactory, does serve to emphasize an economic question which over the years has engaged a very large proportion of economists' attention – that of *resource allocation*. This, for many economists, was and still is *the* economic problem.

The first element in the problem is that we have available in an economy only finite quantities of resources. These may be natural – soil, climate, mineral deposits – which are traditionally termed Land; they may be man-made – factories, machines, roads, etc. – in which case they are referred to as Capital; and then there is man himself – Labour. Land, Labour and Capital, resources which at any given time are strictly limited in supply. They are also capable of being brought together in various combinations to produce alternative types and quantities of goods and services. We are faced with the 'guns or butter' issue of economic choice: the more resources that are used for one particular form of output, the less there are available for others.

This is the basic economic scene. Enter now the actors themselves – consumers jostling to get hold of as many goods and services as they can. Whether it is because we are inherently avaricious or whether it is the nature of our economic system which implants high consumption goals, the shopping list of what consumers would like to have is so long that, to all intents and purposes, we may as well say that wants are unlimited.

(Note that it is the wants of consumers, rather than the needs, with which economics has traditionally been concerned.)

Scarce resources capable of alternative uses – and infinite consumer wants. How can the two be reconciled? The answer is, of course, that they can't. But the aim of economics, according to Robbins, is to make the best of a bad job. The economic problem becomes one of analysing ways of allocating finite resources in such a manner that consumer satisfactions are 'maximized'.

The difficulty is that consumers, except in a very simple economy (for example the croft, where the crofter is both consumer and producer), have no direct relationship with resources. A linking mechanism is needed if the two are to be brought into contact.

There are two very broad alternatives. The first is to interpose between the consumers and resources a central authority with the responsibility for directly planning the types and quantities of goods and services to be produced. There are various criteria by which it could work. The authority could claim to *know* what consumers wanted; it could try to find out – by trial and error, or through the use of market-research techniques; or it could order the production of those goods and services which it thinks consumers need, or *ought* to want. In the rather unattractive extreme form in which it has been presented here, such a system has won the emotive label of a Command Economy. Without going into further detail for the present, it can at least be said that the system would have a more obvious rationale in a poor economy (where basic needs are fairly easily identifiable) than in a richer economy (where production choices may be between sophisticated goods like televisions and washing machines).

The alternative framework for allocating resources is that of the Market Economy, which relies upon the impersonal workings of the price mechanism to do the job of bringing consumers into contact with resources. The intermediary between the two is the firm, which forges a double link, one backward to resources, through the factor market, and the other forward to consumers, in the market for final goods. A market is simply a meeting of buyers and sellers. In the factor market, the so-called 'factors of production' – land, labour and capital – are offered for sale to the various firms competing for their services. The final goods market is that where consumers make their purchases from the variety of goods and services offered for sale by the firms.

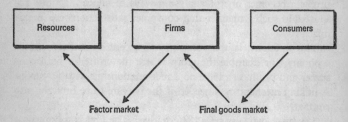

Figure 1

The process has frequently been described as one of economic democracy. Each of the consumers has a limited number of votes, represented by his income. He casts these according to his tastes, for the various candidates (the goods and services on offer) put forward by the firms. The firm is merely a go-between. Having collected the votes, its job is then to re-cast them, on behalf of the consumers, in the market for factors. The more votes it has received from consumers, the greater the quantity of factors it can lay its hands on. For the votes are not an index of the popularity or otherwise of the firms themselves, but rather a signal to them from consumers about how resources should be distributed.

The actual signalling mechanism is provided by movements in relative prices, with the prices of various goods being determined by the forces of supply and demand. Suppose, for example, that two firms each market a thousand potato-peelers, one lot right-handed, the other left-handed. Both charge the same price, 20p. For the right-handed model, the number of consumers willing to buy at that price turns out to be in excess of the number offered for sale. Retailers, to avoid a build-up of queues, raise its price first to 25p, then 30p, until ultimately demand is reduced to match the number they have available. Left-handed potato-peelers, on the other hand, lie unsold on the shelves. In order to clear the stocks, drastic price reductions are offered, presumably tempting the ambidextrous and possibly even inducing normally right-handed peelers to learn to peel left-handedly.

The result is that the receipts of the first manufacturer are increased and those of the other are reduced. The rising prices of right-handed peelers act as a signal to the producer that he should and can secure a greater share of scarce resources. Moreover, his greater profits induce new entrants into the industry – while left-handed peeler producers are meanwhile forced out of business. Ultimately, prices will be stabilized again, but in the process there will have been a shift in resources from the one line of production to the other.

In this system the consumer has dictated everything. Although he has no immediate contact with resources, he has nonetheless managed to direct their use to just those uses which will maximize *his* satisfaction. That is the magic appeal of the market system: that without any planning intervention whatever, consumer demands are met as fully as possible. Everything is achieved through the pulls and pushes of supply and demand forces, Adam Smith's 'invisible hand' directing the whole operation to create an optimal allocation of resources.

However, this optimum will be achieved only if a number of conditions hold good. A very large part of economics has been devoted to establishing just what those conditions would have to be. If prices are to serve their signalling function accurately, they must be precise indicators of, on the one hand, the strength of consumer desires, and, on the other, of the relative scarcity of various resources. Otherwise, consumer votes will not lead to resources being allocated as *they* dictate.

One of these basic conditions is that consumers are able to cast their votes (spend their incomes) rationally and with full knowledge of the 'candidates': if they don't, then there is no guarantee that prices will reflect accurately the relative strengths of consumer demands. It is also necessary that the prices which producers charge are related carefully to the costs of producing additional output. And, finally, the price signals will go un-heeded unless resources can and do freely move from one line of activity to another.

Unfortunately, the working of the price mechanism in practice bears very little resemblance to the ideal economic democracy which we have so far been describing. Consumers are often ignorant – blinded by the technological sophistication of the goods offered, sometimes deceived and pressurized by advertising into mistaken choices. Producers, instead of passing on the votes which they receive into the market for factors may instead pocket some of them for themselves; this happens when they are in a monopolistic position and able to charge excessive prices without fear of retaliation from competitors. And re-sources, particularly labour, may be very slow to respond to the signals of the market. Immobility of resources can mean that the process of adjustment to changing consumer demands may be painfully long-drawn-out.

Much the most undemocratic element in the practical work-ing of the price mechanism is, however, the fact that this is not a system in which there is one man, one vote. Very far from it : with incomes as unequally distributed as they are in this or any other modern capitalist economy, the voting power of different consumers is widely different. Votes from a rich man will carry the same weight in the market as those cast by a poor man despite the fact that a pound spent by a low-income family may represent a much more significant demand decision than that spent by a family which does not have to count the pennies.

All in all, the answer to the question just what prices mean in an economy such as ours is a disturbing one, far from the ideal of matching demand strengths with resource scarcity. Prices are unfortunately to some degree the product of irrational ignorance, excessive producer power and immobility of factors of produc-tion in a highly unequal structure of income distribution. If that is so, price signals are very unreliable indicators, and the alloca-tion of resources which would result from 'leaving things to the market' would be a very different one from the 'optimum' which the system would ideally produce.

These are just some of the limitations of the market mechanism which will be discussed in more detail in later chapters. There is, however, another drawback, much more serious than those listed so far. The Robbins definition of the scope of economics and the type of 'classical' economic analysis on which it was based rested essentially on Adam Smith's presumption that, if each of us resolutely pursues his own self-interest in economic matters, the upshot will be that the general health of the economy as a whole will be simultaneously guaranteed.

But this is not so. The host of individual consumption and production decisions which take place in an unregulated economy is in fact extremely unlikely to add up to the *right total*. If the economy is left entirely to its own devices, its overall behaviour will turn out to be very unsatisfactory. At times, the aggregate of millions of independent decisions will add up to expansionary or inflationary pressures on the economy; at others, they will result in depression and unemployment.

Traditional economics, as we have seen, was essentially concerned with the problem of how resources should be allocated between alternative uses. What it neglected was the question of the general *level* of activity in the economy – whether it was working at full steam or well below its potential capacity. Clearly, concern about the precise allocation of resources between alternative uses – the economics of a little bit more here and a little bit less there – is secondary if a large volume of resources is not being used at all. When much of the economy is lying idle, it makes little sense to concentrate on the problems of scarcity.

And yet this was exactly the position in which economics found itself during the thirties. While teachers of the subject preached to their students the virtues of the unregulated market system and the need to economize here to release resources for deployment there, while economists in official circles held sublimely to the view that full employment was the natural corollary of the market system, millions of ordinary people who had never heard of the theory of Optimum Resource Allocation were thrown out of work. While argument raged between economists on the theoretical niceties of marginal adjustments, the economy moved into a depression which economists knew could not happen.

The problem was that they were in an intellectual straitjacket from which they had the greatest difficulty in extricating themselves. Reluctantly recognizing the reality of mass unemployment, they argued that the fault lay not in the market system but in the imperfections which marred it – governmental interference, trade unions and monopoly. The answers therefore lay in *purifying* the system. In particular, they advocated cutting government expenditure to release resources for private investment, and wage reductions so that firms would be induced to hire more workers.

Unfortunately, these prescriptions were more than just common-room chat, for they were acted on by the government of the day. State spending *was* drastically slashed, even including that on unemployment benefits. The government gave the lead to the private sector by cutting those wage incomes under its own direct control. The 'Geddes Axe' chopped the incomes of teachers, the armed forces and the civil services.

The effect of these measures was simply to make matters worse. Reduced government spending certainly released resources. But would they be used elsewhere? After all, if private firms had wanted to expand production, there were plenty of already unemployed resources there for the asking. What was holding firms back from increasing output wasn't a shortage of labour and capital but doubt about whether they could *sell* any more in an economy with three million unemployed.

Cutting wages in such circumstances could hardly be the answer either. For an individual firm it might just work. A cut in wage-rates might, if the firm was boldly optimistic about its prospects, represent a reduction in costs sufficient to induce it to produce more and employ additional workers. But if *all* wages were cut at the same time, spending in the economy would be correspondingly reduced; the purchasing power to buy the increased output simply wouldn't be there. As Joan Robinson once put it, the effect is analogous to the man going to watch a procession who takes with him a box to stand on. If he is the only one who does so, he *will* get a better view. But if everyone takes along a box, they are back where they started from.

Fortunately, the solution was in the making. John Maynard Keynes was giving birth to a work which he described, in a letter to George Bernard Shaw, as 'a book on economic theory which will largely revolutionize – not, I suppose, at once but in the course of the next ten years – the way the world thinks about economic problems'. With the publication of his *General Theory of Employment, Interest and Money* in 1936, Keynes finally achieved the intellectual somersault needed to convert the vicious circle of his times into a potentially virtuous one. For many years he had been struggling intuitively against economic ortho-doxy before he succeeded in articulating the causes of cyclical unemployment and what it was about an unregulated market system which made recurring unemployment near-inevitable. In retrospect, it is all very simple.

The key to increased employment, argued Keynes, lay in more spending. The unemployment of the thirties was tragically paradoxical. The workers were there, the capital was there. The workers wanted jobs, the producers wanted profit. There was no immediate conflict of interest. The missing ingredient was simply the wherewithal to buy any increase in output. *Anything*, said Keynes, which raises demand in the economy will contribute to reducing unemployment. If you like, employ men to dig holes in the ground and fill them up again. Pay them incomes. What will they do with them? They will go out and spend the greater part – on food, clothes, beer, paying bills. The recipients of such payments would, in turn, undertake further spending themselves, and a cumulative process of income expansion would begin, drawing into employment more and more hitherto unemployed resources.

Hole-digging, although it would do the trick, is an un-imaginative and unproductive way of stimulating an economy. How much more sensible for the government to create incomes by spending on socially worthwhile projects like road-building or slum clearance, and ultimately to restore the confidence of private entrepreneurs. Once that happens they will invest in new factories and machines, producing goods to meet the demands of consumers whose incomes have been increased by being absorbed again into the active work-force.

But where is the money to come from to pay for such a grandiose design? It is very difficult for the non-economist (and it was also difficult for economists at that time) to realize that shortage of money can never be a constraint for governments in a modern economy. Money, although it means so much to us as individuals, is only a lubricator of the economic system; what matters is the volume of real things – goods and services – which the economy is able to produce. The money supply is in the hands of the government, which controls the printing presses. If, in conditions of full employment, it doubles the quantity of money by handing us all out a bonus equivalent to our present incomes, we certainly won't be twice as well off as a result. When we try to spend our increased incomes, we will come across the problem that there are no more goods available in the shops. Our increased purchasing power, in those circumstances, may merely push up prices. But when there is mass unemployment, the situation is a very different one. In this case, spending a hand-out from the State soon leads to a feed-back to producers, who rush to employ labour and other resources to meet our increased demands.

What was needed, claimed Keynes, was a combination of various measures. The government could try to snap the private sector out of its depression, by offering tax cuts (to both firms and consumers), lower interest rates and subsidies of one kind and another. Or the government could undertake the job of expanding demand itself. If the private sector was sticky, the government itself should operate as the big spender, knowing that sooner or later private firms would respond to the increased market for their goods which such a policy would produce. Stimulate the private sector, 'pump-prime' it through government spending – and, if necessary, persist with compensatory expenditure by the State to make good the deficiencies of private firms. This was the sort of package which Keynes recommended, and each of its ingredients was directly opposite to the recommendations of the orthodox economists who had previously held the stage.

Such iconoclastic advice, however, went against the grain for two reasons. The first was that it was contrary to all the canons of 'sound finance' on which governmental economics had been built since the days of Gladstone. The function of the Treasury, it was held, was essentially one of good housekeeping. In the same way as you or I know that we must keep our spending in line with income if we are to avoid the attentions of the Official Receiver, so a government which disburses more than it receives in taxation will also end up in Queer Street, having meanwhile 'put the country in the red'. But this, like the argument about wage cuts, is an example of the fallacy of composition: what is true of the parts need not necessarily be true of the whole. If *you* get into debt, spend more than your income, then it will be to another individual or bank who will ultimately demand repayment and put the pressure on. But if your debt is to another member of your family, then – whatever the domestic acrimony which it causes – the family itself will be neither worse off nor better off than before. It is an internal book-keeping transaction between the members.

Similarly, if the government spends more than it receives in taxes – by, for example, borrowing from the general public – then, provided it doesn't involve foreigners, its increased indebtedness is a domestic matter between members of the national family which it represents. The economy as a whole is neither richer nor poorer than before. But if the effect of government borrowing from one section of the community to finance higher spending is that unemployment is reduced and output increased, the economy *will* be better off than before. With the higher tax revenues which will result from increased incomes, the original borrowing can, if so desired, be repaid. Deficit financing in a depression, far from being profligate extravagance, is straightforward common sense.

The other reason why contemporaries found it so difficult to swallow the Keynesian prescription was that it represented a political attack on a hallowed orthodoxy. The essence of the Keynesian message was that a totally unregulated, laisser-faire, free-enterprise economy simply could not be relied upon to do the job of creating and maintaining full employment. If the degradation and sheer waste of unemployment was ever to be eliminated, the State would have to accept explicit responsibility for achieving that objective. Moreover, the means which it would have to use represented a quite unprecedented degree of interference in the everyday workings of the economy. Business could no longer be left to businessmen; what was required was a substantial circumscription of their actions, manipulation of their behaviour in order to yield the right overall result. What had been widely dubbed as 'meddling' or 'interference' in the past would now have to be sold as paternalistic intervention.

It was a bitter pill. The idea that State management of the economy was an essential means to the widely willed end of full employment was highly unpalatable. But Keynes was no Marxist extremist. 'Even if we need a religion, how can we find it in the rabid rubbish of the Red bookshops? It is hard for an educated, decent, intelligent son of Western Europe to find his ideals here, unless he has first suffered some strange and horrid process of conversion which has changed all his values.' [1] Keynes's values *hadn't* been transformed by his economic discoveries. 'I can be influenced by what seems to be justice and good sense; but the *class* war will find me on the side of the educated *bourgeoisie*.' [2] For Keynes, his theory was 'moderately conservative in its implications. For whilst it indicates the vital importance of establishing certain central controls in matters which are now left in the main to individual initiative, there are wide fields of activity which are unaffected.' [3] Keynes, coming as he did from the great liberal tradition, saw that a more active interventionist policy on the part of government was the only way in which that tradition could be preserved. The old order, capitalism itself, could survive only with this major modification.

Keynes was too late to avert the tragedy of the inter-war years. By the time that his ideas had filtered through into official orthodoxy, the unemployment which had bedevilled western economies had started to solve itself. Hitler had begun to show

1. J. M. Keynes, *Essays in Persuasion*, Macmillan, 1931.
2. ibid.
3. J. M. Keynes, *The General Theory of Employment, Interest and Money*, Macmillan, 1936, pp. 377–8.

the way in Nazi Germany, his policy of massive arms build-up incidentally providing the level of spending needed to create jobs for all. It was even worse than Keynes's joke about digging holes, but technically it was sufficient. Soon, the other major powers followed suit, and the rational application of Keynesian techniques to achieve full employment by conscious manipulation of economic variables had to wait till the post-war years. In Chapter 3, we will look at the Keynesian approach in more detail. We shall then have to ask how successful it has been in practice.

3

The Economic Mechanism

Why were the orthodox economists of the inter-war years so blind to the most pressing problem of their times? In what sort of intellectual stranglehold were they which made it so difficult for them even to conceive of a situation of mass unemployment, let alone provide a solution to it? Setting out the logic of the so-called 'classical' position shows just how great an upheaval in economic thinking Keynes brought about.

Discovering what determines the level of employment in an economy is a highly complex matter. We shall have to resort to the economist's irritating but useful trick of starting with a very simplified 'model' of the economy, and adding more realistic complications stage by stage.

Imagine, then, an economy in which there is no foreign trade (a 'closed' economy), and in which there is no governmental economic activity. In this economy, we shall focus on the behaviour of two very broad groups – households and firms. Firms are the producing units in the economy. They hire the services of people from the households, put them to work in their factories and produce goods which they then sell to households in their capacity as consumers. Households, on the other hand, are the places where people live, eat, drink and make love. They are also the source of the economy's labour supply and the purchasers of national output. The relationships between households and firms can be illustrated in a simple 'circular flow' diagram.

Fig. 2A shows the material interdependence between the two. From households to firms, there is a flow of factor services as the working population offers itself for hire in the firms' factories. And from firms to households there is a flow of goods

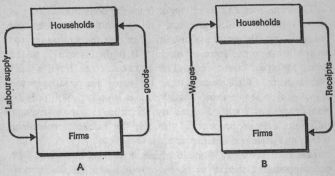

Figure 2

which the firms have produced with the help of the labour force. Corresponding to these physical flows are financial relationships between firms and households shown in Fig. 2B. These monetary flows are in the reverse direction to the physical flows. Thus there are payments, firstly from firms to households in the form of wages, and secondly from households to firms, firms' receipts resulting from the sale of their goods.

Just one more simplifying, if absurd, assumption, and we can put our basic economy to work. Suppose that people, when they get their wages, spend them wholly and immediately on goods – they save nothing at all. Then if the value of output produced by the firms happens to be, say, £1,000, the economy will operate as in Fig. 3.

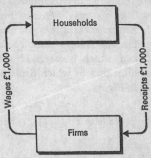

Figure 3

The firms hire £1,000 of labour from the households, and pay out a wage bill of that amount. The households then use those wages to buy the output of the firms, so that the £1,000 returns to the firms in the form of receipts. It is then available to the firms to repeat the process. The £1,000 income level is self-perpetuating. (This assumes that the firms are producing the goods which people *want*. Mistakes, it is supposed, will only be temporary and soon corrected by shifts in resources between different lines of production through the market mechanism which was discussed in Chapter 2.)

This basic economy is one in which, if we label income Y, and consumption C, then Y = C. Its only use is to emphasize one very important point. That is, what are costs to the firms are incomes to households. Therefore, since the firms sell their output at prices which are made up of their various costs, the income of households (which are costs looked at from a different viewpoint) is always sufficient for them to buy the firms' output in its entirety.

The level of income and output in this basic economy is obviously stable. There is no reason why it should ever deviate from £1,000. But what determines the level of *employment* in such a system? The answer, and this is really the classical argument, is that employment will depend on the *wage rate* – which in turn is the result of the forces of supply and demand in the labour market.

By and large, it is safe to generalize that the higher the wage rate, the more workers will offer themselves for hire. Firms, on the other hand, will see matters differently. For them, the higher the wage rate, the fewer workers they are prepared to take on. Taking three possible wage rates – £10, £20 and £30 a week – the amount of labour which households would be willing to supply and the amount of jobs which firms would be prepared to offer might be as in Fig. 3.

Table 1

Wage rate	Supply of labour	Jobs offered
£10	250	750
£20	500	500
£30	750	250

Precisely the same information can be shown in a graphical form (Fig. 4).

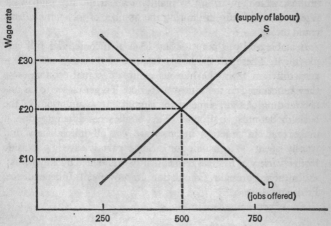

Figure 4

What becomes clear is that there is only *one* wage rate at which the amount of services which households are prepared to offer is compatible with the amount of jobs which the firms are willing to create. That 'equilibrium' wage rate is obviously £20 a week. At £30, the supply of labour will exceed the demand for it; at £10, the number of jobs offered will be greater than the number of people offering themselves for hire.

When we talk of unemployment, we generally refer to that which is involuntary – people without jobs who would be willing to accept work at the going rate. Provided that wage rates are flexible, unemployment in this sense can exist in our basic economy only temporarily, as a result of the wage rate rising above the equilibrium level. As soon as the excess of supply over demand forces it down again, the market for labour will clear itself in just the same way that the market for oranges does.

This is just what the classical economists were saying about the thirties. The dreadful unemployment of that time, they argued, arose principally because wage rates were too high. If only they could be cut, there would be jobs for everyone who wanted them. And what stopped them falling naturally was the existence of a major imperfection in the labour market – trade unions, which, in trying to maintain an artificially high wage rate, succeeded only in limiting the number of jobs which firms could create.

A stable and self-perpetuating level of income, and full employment. These are the happy features of the basic economy – very different from the hideous reality of actual economies as they functioned in the inter-war period. To get closer to an understanding of *that*, some of the simplifying assumptions of the basic model must be dropped. First of all, what difference does it make that, in practice, incomes are *not* all immediately and wholly spent on consumption? Some part is saved, put aside from a variety of motives resplendently catalogued by Keynes as: Precaution, Foresight, Calculation, Improvement, Independence, Pride and Avarice.[1]

The effect can be seen in Fig. 5.

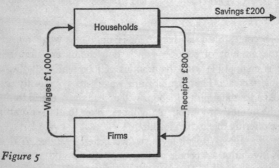

Figure 5

Savings – £200 in this case – represents a leakage from the circular flow. It is £200 which does *not* return to the firms. And since the receipts of the firms are what they use to pay for workers, the number which they are able to hire is correspondingly reduced. As a result of their saving, households will thus find themselves at the next stage with reduced incomes of only £800. If their savings behaviour is stable – if, that is, we suppose that

1. J. M. Keynes, *General Theory of Employment, Interest and Money*, p. 108.

they will always try to save one fifth of their incomes – then the consequences are startling indeed. The next few stages in the process are summarized in Fig. 6, showing reduced receipts to

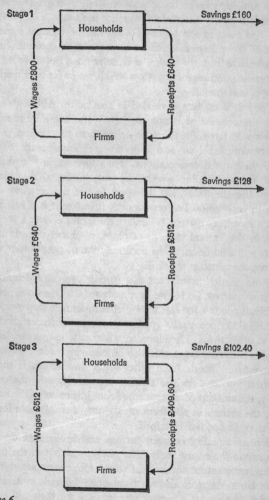

Figure 6

the firms and therefore reduced incomes to the people – of £640, £512 and £409.60.

The final outcome of this process is predictable. Receipts to firms and incomes to households will fall to zero! Our attempt to explain reality has clearly overshot the mark. Things weren't *that* bad even in the 1930s. To redress the balance somewhat, another complication needs to be taken into account. Savings are a leakage from the system of circular flow. But there is also an important *injection* into the flow which has so far been neglected. That is, investment.

A word of caution is needed at this point. Although economists are accused of jargonizing, they also use a large number of everyday terms. But they re-define them to serve the purpose of economic analysis and give them meaning quite different from their usual connotations. Thus 'investment' in ordinary usage means building society deposits, holdings of stocks and shares and the like. That, however, is not the meaning of the term in economics. For economists, investment is a *real* rather than a monetary matter. It denotes the increase, over a period of time, in the 'capital stock' – of plant, machinery, roads and so on. It is the addition to the accumulation of past output which was not consumed at the time.

In our model, investment is a further source of demand for the firms' output. So far we have assumed that the firms produce only final goods – for sale to households. In fact, however, some firms will produce *capital* goods rather than consumer goods, for sale to other firms. Therefore, in addition to consumer demand from households, firms will also be receiving orders for capital or investment goods from other firms. Investment is thus an *injection* into the circular flow of income. If, as is the case in Fig. 7, the amount of investment (£200) just matches the leakage from the system in the form of savings, then a stable level of income of £1,000 is maintained.

Such an equality between savings and investment does not seem *prima facie* very likely. The problem is that in the model, and to some extent in the real world too, savers are different people from investors and act from quite different motivations. Individuals save for a variety of reasons – for their old age, to

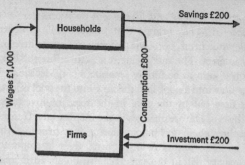

Figure 7

get married, to buy a new car, to guard against a rainy day. Investment, on the other hand, is undertaken by firms intent upon building up their capacity to meet some expected increase in demand in the future and to profit from it. Since savings and investment decisions are made from different motives by different people unaware of the actions of others, there is no reason at all why what one group plan to save will be precisely matched by what the other group plan to invest. (Although there will be overlapping: firms themselves may save to finance their own investment, and to that extent the two sets of decisions are kept in line.)

The consequences of the highly probable disparity between savings and investment plans are far-reaching. If the amount which households plan to save exceeds the amount which firms plan to invest, the result will be similar to that illustrated in Fig. 5 (where savings happened to be £200 and investment zero). There will be a *downward* pressure on the level of income. If, on the other hand, firms plan to invest (and do so on the basis of bank credit) more than households plan to save, the effect will be for incomes and output to be pushed up.

We therefore have all the ingredients here for an unstable economy, with income and output fluctuating in response to changing savings and investment plans. How could the classicists claim that such an economy would automatically regulate itself towards full employment stability? Once again, their answer was that market forces would do the job.

For them, savings and investment decisions were *not* entirely unconnected. They argued that people saved in order to earn interest while firms, borrowing money to finance investment, had to *pay* interest. The rate of interest is therefore the link between what only seem to be totally separate sets of decisions. In effect, savings flow into a pool, and the flow into the pool is just matched by the flow out of the pool in the form of investment. What keeps them in line are changes in the interest rate. If, for example, a breakthrough in technology means that firms see the opportunity of more profitable investment, their attempts to expand their capacity will at the same time stimulate an increase in the amount that people save. As firms try to borrow funds, competition between them forces up the rate of interest and induces the appropriate response from households. The flow between firms and households remains unbroken according to the classical line of reasoning illustrated in Fig. 8.

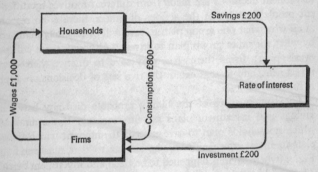

Figure 8

This, then, was the powerful theoretical standpoint of the pre-Keynesian economists. Unimpeded market forces would not only secure an optimal allocation of scarce resources. They would also ensure that the economy would be self-equilibrating at a level of full employment. If unemployment *did* occur, as in the interwar years, it was due to imperfections in the market. The classical prescriptions followed logically from their analysis of the problem. In particular they advocated reduction of wage rates, and encouragement of saving to provide resources for new investment which would get the economy moving again.

The Keynesian attack on the classical position was directed against a vital link in the chain of argument – the role of the rate of interest in keeping savings and investment plans in line with each other. For Keynes, the notion that interest is primarily the reward for abstinence, and that the level of savings which people plan to undertake is chiefly determined by the rate of interest, were both manifestly implausible propositions. If, for example, you save by putting part of your weekly income under the floor-boards, you earn no interest as a result. Interest only becomes payable when you part with your savings and exchange them for an asset other than money. In Keynesian jargon, interest is the return for forfeiting liquidity – for holding savings in a form other than money – rather than the reward for saving as such. Moreover, the principal determinant of savings, according to Keynes, is not the rate of interest but the level of income. If someone has an income of £20 a week and the rate of interest on building society deposits rises from 6 to 7 per cent, he is not likely to increase his savings very much or even at all; on the other hand, a rise in his income from £20 to £30 may well get him putting more aside each week.

These were the broad lines of the Keynesian critique of the classical interest-rate theory. The importance of his attack was that, once he could show that interest rates were not capable of bringing .savings and investment plans into compatibility, the economy lost its automatic full-employment stability. If the flow of savings into the pool of loanable funds is not matched by the flow out into investment by changes in interest rates, then it is likely that plans to save will constantly diverge from plans to investment – with the upward and downward pressures on the level of income which we have already seen to be the consequence. Planned savings exceeding planned investment – leakages being greater than injections into the circular flow – will reduce income. Planned investment exceeding planned savings will cause income to rise.

But these upward and downward movements of income do not go on for ever. They are finite. And the way in which originally disparate plans to save and invest are ultimately made compatible is explained by the theory of the Multiplier.

Suppose that, to begin with, the level of income has settled at £1,000, with savings and investment plans coincidentally equal at £200. For some reason or other, people now propose to become more thrifty. In the future they decide that they will save 25 per cent of their incomes rather than 20 per cent. Savings therefore increase to £250 in the first place (Fig. 9), and the original balance of the economy is destroyed.

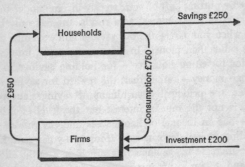

Figure 9

What is the result? Initially, only £750 comes back to the firms as receipts, and this, together with continued investment demand of £200, is the basis of income at the next stage being reduced to £950. That, however, is not the end of the story. If, despite their lower income, people continue to try to save 25 per cent, they will set aside some £237.50 at this stage. Consumption will consequently be reduced to £712.50 and that is the amount which returns to the firms as receipts. Added to investment demand of £200, it means that what flows back to households as incomes falls once again – to £912.50 (Fig. 10).

Income will continue to fall, but the fall at each stage is getting smaller and smaller. We can predict the final outcome. The slide in income will stop only when savings are ultimately brought into line with investment. With firms continuing to invest £200, the question which we have to ask is, 'At what level of income will people plan to save only that amount?' Since we have

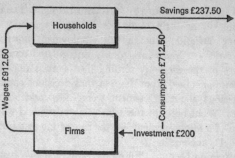

Figure 10

assumed that their savings propensity is stable at 25 per cent, the answer is obviously £800. That indeed is where the decline in income will be halted. Planned savings will be £200 and since they just match planned investment a new 'equilibrium' will have been established (Fig. 11).

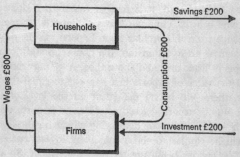

Figure 11

At this stage, until planned savings or investment happen to change again, the income level will remain stable. But it is 20 per cent below the original level – and it may be expected that employment will have fallen similarly. The great Keynesian breakthrough was to show just this: that there is not, as the classicists held, a single unique equilibrium at the level of full employment, but that there are an infinite number of equilibria

related to different savings and investment plans. The depressed
conditions of the early 1930s, for example, were not merely a
temporary deviation from a full employment norm, but the
natural order of things in a totally unregulated economy. The
possibility of the economy settling into a mass unemployment
equilibrium stemmed from the fact that decisions about savings
and decisions about investment were independent and uncoordinated. What brought them into line in the end was not the
variation of a minor element like the rate of interest, but changes
in the level of income itself.

- The situation becomes still more complex if two further simplifying assumptions which we made at the outset are now
dropped. We have been discussing the working of an economy
without government economic activity and without foreign trade.
Both, however, can be fairly easily integrated into the circular
flow analysis.

Take foreign trade to begin with. If, when they receive their
incomes, households choose to spend part of them on goods
imported from abroad, it is foreign rather than domestic producers who benefit. Thus purchases of imports represent a further leakage from the circular flow. Exports, on the other hand,
can be seen as an injection into the flow – an additional source
of receipts to firms over and above those resulting from domestic
sales. If the value of exports just happens to equal the value of
imports, there will be no net effect on the level of domestic
income. But if exports exceed imports, or imports exceed exports, the expansionary or depressing effects on the level of income will be similar to those caused by investment exceeding
savings, or savings being greater than investment. So also with
government. Taxes on the community are a leakage from the
circular flow of income – they are no longer available for private
consumption or investment purposes and are a destruction of
purchasing power. Government expenditure, on the other hand,
is an injection into the system, a further element in aggregate
demand. Fig. 12 shows the place of these additional leakages and
injections in the circular flow.

It can be seen from Fig. 12 that the condition necessary for
maintaining any given level of income in the economy now needs

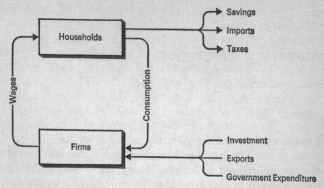

Figure 12

restating. Instead of an equality between planned saving and planned investment, the condition now becomes:

Planned leakages (savings plus imports plus taxes) must = Planned injections (investment plus exports plus government expenditure).

So far as the private sector is concerned, there is no reason why savings plans should automatically match investment plans, or that import demand should equal export demand. Hence, if the government follows Gladstonian principles in balancing its budget (keeping expenditure in line with its income from taxes), the result will almost always be that the level of income in the economy is rising or falling.

It was the achievement of Keynes to show that a stable level of national income requires positive government intervention. Moreover, Keynes demonstrated that stability as such is not the appropriate target – for it can occur at any one of a number of income and employment levels. *Full employment*, far from being a natural outcome of the workings of an unrestricted market mechanism, can be achieved only by deliberate management of the economy in a way which was anathema to economists and politicians of the pre-war period. In Chapter 4, we examine the tools which government has at its disposal to do the job.

4

Managing the Economy

Keynes was too late to solve the problems of the inter-war years. By the time his ideas had gained acceptance and filtered through into official orthodoxy, Britain was at war again. In 1944, however, looking forward to the end of hostilities and determined to avoid the economic disasters which had followed the First World War, the government in a historic White Paper committed itself for the first time to securing 'a high and stable level of employment'. The very fact that a government was prepared to take on this responsibility reflected a confidence that in principle Keynes had cracked the nut of mass unemployment, and that full employment could be attained by conscious manipulation of the economic system by the State. Moreover, an incidental by-product of the more highly controlled wartime economy was that a mass of economic data – concerning national income, investment and consumption – had become available for the first time and could serve as the basis for managing the economy along Keynesian lines.

The problem, as we have seen, is that an unregulated economy is extremely unlikely to hit full employment, except temporarily and by chance. The reason for this is that the constituents of aggregate demand – consumption, investment and the foreign trade surplus – are determined by millions of largely independent decisions taken by individuals and firms in an uncoordinated fashion. The probability is that they will add up to a total demand either greater or less than that needed to purchase the output which would be produced at full employment. The sort of unemployment which Keynes was primarily concerned with (and there are others which we shall examine later) was that caused simply by demand-deficiency, a shortfall in spending by the private sector. Hence the equally simple solution – to increase the total spending in the economy to the appropriate level.

In essence, the process of demand management of the economy boils down to two stages – diagnosis and action. The first task of the authorities is to form a view of the productive capability of the economy. If all resources were fully utilized, what would be the value of the resulting output of goods and services? Suppose that the answer which they give is, say, £50,000 million. Next they must inquire what the probable level of demand in the economy will be on the assumption that the government takes no further action. Suppose that their estimates suggest a situation like that illustrated in Fig. 13. Determining the total demand for

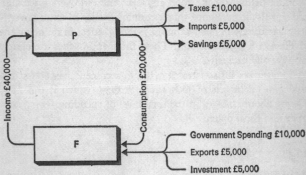

Figure 13

the coming period involves looking at its components and forecasting the amounts of the various leakages and injections in the circular flow. In this particular case, the government starts from a position in which its budget is balanced, receipts from taxes equalling disbursements at £10,000 million. The figure for private consumption, it has estimated, will be £20,000 million. Exports are forecast as equalling imports at £5,000 million, and savings and investment are also balanced at the same figure.

This is in fact a very simple case, with each of the leakages happening to match a corresponding injection. The economy is therefore in an equilibrium position. The only problem is that the total level of demand which is generated amounts to only

£40,000 million, £10,000 million short of the spending required to buy the output which would result from full employment of resources.

So much for diagnosis. What can the authorities do about it? If full employment is to be achieved, they must somehow fill the so-called 'deflationary gap' – and ensure that spending in fact turns out to be £50,000 million rather than the £40,000 which will be spent if nothing is done.

Broadly, the government can adopt one of three approaches. Firstly, it can work on the private sector to revise its plans – take measures to stimulate consumption, investment and exports. Secondly, it may despair of the private sector and adjust its own spending plans to make good any deficiency in overall demand. And thirdly, it may hope that a certain amount of extra government spending will have a 'pump-priming' effect in inducing the private sector to follow suit. These three approaches are clearly not mutually exclusive.

Whatever its broad strategy, the government has at its disposal two major sets of techniques through which it can hope to bring about changes in the total level of spending – monetary policy and fiscal policy.

Monetary Policy

Monetary policy can take a variety of forms. (i) The government can pin its hopes on controlling the *total supply of money* in the economy in the belief that there is some causal relationship between this particular variable and the level of demand. (ii) Its objective may, on the other hand, be to control the availability and use of particular types of credit – like *bank advances* or *hire purchase*. (iii) And finally it might be essentially concerned with the price of money and credit – trying to bring about a certain structure of *interest rates* in the economy. Of these three, only the last two are strictly 'Keynesian' techniques. The other, which sees the total money supply as the key variable, is a throwback to the pre-Keynesian 'Quantity Theory' thinking which has been resurrected in recent years, particularly by Professor Milton Friedman of Chicago, who detects a close correlation between money supply and the level of economic activity and concludes that controlling the money supply is a sufficient basis for an otherwise self-regulating economy. Discussion of this 'Monetarist' view is postponed to Chapter 6, which deals with inflation. For now, we shall concentrate on the Keynesian weapons themselves.

In principle, Keynesian techniques are decidedly gentlemanly. They consist of *general* manipulation of the major variables in the economy rather than specific and selective direct controls. Thus, one of the virtues traditionally claimed for monetary policy – and this is perhaps why it has had particular appeal to more right-wing governments – is that it operates anonymously through the market system and is administered at the grass roots level by the banking and credit institutions rather than by the government itself. Having set the general scene through its control over the Bank of England, the government can then sit back and watch the details of its policy be etched out through the relationships of the central bank with other financial institutions. That, at least, is the theory. In practice, the history of monetary policy in the post-war years consists largely of a search by governments to evolve tighter techniques of control in face of equally persistent attempts to avoid such controls by an ever proliferating number of financial agencies. Increasingly, the authorities have had to rely upon more or less direct instructions to the different parts of the financial sector to toe the official monetary line. This is not the place to chart the arid course of shifting emphasis on cash ratios, liquidity ratios, bank rate, special deposits and the like. Suffice it to say that the governmental authorities have less than total and immediate control over the financial institutions, not least because the Bank of England, despite its nationalization, has been remarkably successful in maintaining a posture often distinctly independent from that of the government of the day.

Our concern here is more with the general effectiveness of monetary policy. The object of the exercise is to influence the components of aggregate demand in the economy – in particular, consumption and investment spending. Take first interest-rate policy – manipulation of the price of credit by the central authorities. This might be hoped to affect both consumption and

investment plans as individuals and firms adjust their intended
spending to changes in the cost of borrowing funds. But does it
work? In the light of post-war experience, there has been increasing scepticism about just how sensitive consumers and
firms are to interest rates. And secondly, to the extent that they do
respond, there is the question of who is likely to be most
affected.

Consumption certainly does not seem to be very responsive to
changes in the cost of borrowing. Consider, for example, the decision to buy a new car. How many customers are likely to be
deterred by a rise in interest rates? For most people, perhaps
ignorant anyway of the true interest rate which they are being
asked to pay, deposit requirements and repayment periods are
likely to be far more important considerations.

And what about businessmen? How far do *they* take into
account a rise in the cost of borrowing when they are deciding
whether or not to invest in new plant and machinery? Once
again, it is doubtful if interest-cost is a major factor in the investment decision. There are a number of reasons for this. A
good deal of industry is largely self-financing, not greatly dependent on outside sources of funds. Interest costs are generally
dwarfed by annual capital repayments given the short 'pay-off'
periods at which most manufacturing industry aims. The impact
of rising interest rates is cushioned in an inflationary situation
in which higher charges can be fairly easily passed on to the
consumer. Investment plans tend to be part of a long-term
strategy which it is difficult to adjust in response to short-term
changes. And what above all counts for firms is the way in which
they view their future prospects. If they are optimistic about
coming expansion, they will go ahead with investment despite
increased interest charges. If they are pessimistic, lower interest
rates are unlikely to improve their confidence.

Of course, the success of interest-rate policy in influencing
investment depends on the *amount* by which rates are changed.
And here is a great weakness of this type of monetary policy. A
sharp and substantial increase in the interest rate may well succeed in reducing investment spending. But it will work only by
shaking industry's confidence in the future economic outlook.

The trouble is that, once shaken, confidence may prove extremely difficult to restore. The problem, then, is that interest-rate signals tend to be either ignored or taken altogether too seriously. That is why one commentator has concluded that such policy is either 'useless or vicious'.[1]

Nor is there any reason for modifying this conclusion when we look at the question of who is most likely to be affected by interest changes. It is the enterprises most dependent on external finance: small firms, those engaged in long-term projects like building and fast-growing firms). The impact of interest-rate policy is in fact highly selective and it is by no means obvious that the areas in which it is likely to have most effect are those which the authorities would wish to bear the brunt of their financial discipline.

Increasingly during the post-war years governments came to exercise the other type of monetary influence – control over particular sorts of credit such as bank advances and hire purchase. The logic of limiting bank credit is appealingly straightforward. If the money just isn't there, then surely spending must be cut? But, here again, major problems have arisen for the authorities. Quite apart from the question of whether the selective administration of credit squeezes is a matter appropriately left to bank managers, the difficulty has been that, in a sophisticated financial sector such as exists in a modern economy, there are many ways round official constraints. Putting the pressure on one part of the market merely forces potential borrowers to seek funds elsewhere, and there are various alternative sources available – insurance companies, finance houses, extended trade credit and so on. What is worse, extension of the official network of constraint to include these alternatives tends to result in the proliferation of still more institutions working in a way designed to sidestep official pressure. Hire purchase controls, on the other hand – although they too can to some extent be circumvented – certainly have been effective in short-term demand management. However, their impact is a narrow one on consumer-good manufacturers like the car industry, who can

1. R. Opie, 'The Future of Monetary Policy', in *Unfashionable Economics*, ed. P. P. Streeten, Weidenfeld & Nicolson, 1970, p. 273.

reasonably complain that their development has been stunted by their being *used* as an instrument of government policy.

All in all, the history of monetary policy during the post-war years has been a disappointment to its devotees. Far from being an anonymous, non-selective and delicate instrument of control, it has turned out to be blunt, harshly discriminative and difficult to administer effectively. Sometimes it has failed to work at all, sometimes it has succeeded by clumsy overkill and revealed a further defect – its irreversibility. As an element in the Keynesian battery of demand-management techniques it must now surely be relegated to a minor role subordinate to the other major weapon of fiscal policy.

Fiscal Policy

The government's ability to tax the community and to spend on its behalf gives it a major lever on the level of activity in the economy. Particular taxes and forms of spending can be adjusted to influence private consumption and investment. And there is also the impact on the economy of the budget – how much the government spends in relation to how much it receives in taxation.

Supposing, then, that there is substantial unemployment in the economy, what is the proper fiscal approach? First of all, this is clearly a time for cutting taxes on individuals and firms, in the hope of inducing them to increase their spending plans. In particular, the authorities should aim at redistributing income from those who tend to save a large proportion of their incomes in favour of those with a high propensity to consume. There is more to it than that. After all, cutting taxes helps only those individuals and firms who are *paying* taxes. For those who aren't, an additional way of stimulating spending is for the government to hand out higher unemployment benefits, larger family allowances and investment grants to firms to help them in installing new plant and equipment. The government itself can to some extent compensate for the failure of the private sector to generate sufficient purchasing power to absorb full employment output. It can expand the output of public enterprises and increase other types of spending under its direct control – public-works programmes of road, hospital, school and house-building; it can build new factories and offer them to the private sector on favourable terms.

But who is to foot the bill? If the government is to spend more than it takes in from taxes, it will have to borrow or resort to the printing press to finance its deficit.

Such an approach seems to the layman and seemed, too, to the politicians and economists of the thirties as irresponsible in the extreme. To suggest that the appropriate policy was for governments consciously to encourage an abandonment of thrift, deliberately to get themselves into debt, appeared the height of profligacy – a policy which might possibly have a short-term effect in stimulating demand but which was bound to lead to national bankruptcy in the long-run.

In fact, the opposite is the nearer to the truth. Deficit financing stands a good chance of being *self*-financing. If, on Keynesian lines, it succeeds in getting the economy moving again, then output and income begin to rise. Even with unchanged tax *rates*, the tax *receipts* accruing to the government will automatically increase and be available, if so desired, for repaying the initial borrowings.

The role of taxation in 'functional finance' is a difficult one for the individual to understand. For most taxpayers, the purpose of taxation is simply to raise money for financing governmental spending. They may fear that some of it goes down the drain of governmental extravagance and waste. They may admit that much of it pays for a variety of useful services. But, in fact, this is only part of the story. For if we take the opposite situation to that of the thirties and look at an economy in which total spending plans seem likely to exceed the value of full employment output, then part of the purpose of taxation is quite simply to destroy purchasing power. A government faced with an *inflationary* gap increases taxes – not to increase its own expenditure but to *stop* a certain amount of spending.

Very broadly, then, a government faced with excess demand can be expected to budget for a surplus; if there is not enough demand being generated, a deficit is called for. In other words, a budget surplus is not, as many people still think, a sign that things are going rather well. A surplus may be evidence that the economy is out of balance just as much as a budget deficit (which many people still think indicates that the government has somehow got its sums wrong). The budget is a major weapon in the Keynesian armoury for adjusting the amount of spending in the economy to the desired level.

The Limits of Keynes

How effective have the Keynesian tricks proved to be when applied by successive post-war governments? A quick glance at the economic record suggests that they have worked very well, with the economy running at a very much higher and consistent level of employment than it managed before the war. However, during the post-war years there have also been a number of propitious forces at work which, even if the Keynesian lessons had never been learned, would have kept economies much more buoyant. The conjunction of large-scale government spending on defence and social services, the massive increase in foreign trade which followed on the gradual liberalization of the international trading system, and a rapid rate of technological progress must all have helped to stimulate economic activity and keep up employment.

Nevertheless, *one* of the reasons for near-full employment has been that governments have put it high in their list of policy objective with a priority which was only meaningful given a Keynesian understanding of the nature and causes of unemployment. In the absence of the Keynesian breakthrough, governments may have resorted to deflationary policies (to cure, for example, balance of payments deficits) to an even greater extent than they have. It is on this basis that Professor R. C. O. Matthews concludes: 'In this way the tendency for demand to be high for reasons independent of government action would have been checked by government action. That this was not done is something for which economists and the Keynesian revolution can take some credit.'[2]

2. R. C. O. Matthews, 'Why has Britain had Full Employment since the War?' *Economic Journal*, September 1968, p. 569.

Keynesianism works – that is the lesson of the post-war success of industrial economies in avoiding the horrors of mass unemployment and extreme business fluctuations. But what we have also learned are the *limitations* of demand management. There are three basic weaknesses of the Keynesian approach which can be outlined at this stage before we go on to elaborate them in subsequent chapters.

(i) Firstly, there are the crudities of the fiscal and monetary techniques themselves, and of the economic forecasting on the basis of which they are used. The ideal instrument for managing the level of demand in the economy should have four main qualities. First, we need to know the *direction* in which it will work – that pulling one lever will have an expansionary effect, while pulling another will dampen the economy down. Second, the *amount* of change must be predictable; the Keynesian 'multiplier' needs to be known so that we can be sure that the effect of policy on total demand is neither too great nor too small. Thirdly, *timing* is also vital; exactly when is the policy impact going to take place? And finally, the ideal instrument of control would be capable of working in both directions and be rapidly reversible.

Clearly both monetary and fiscal policy as they have operated in the post-war years fall very short of these ideal criteria. By and large, the direction in which they are likely to work *is* predictable (although even here it may be uncertain whether a given rise in personal taxes will affect consumption or be met out of reduced savings, or whether high marginal rates of taxation will increase or reduce the willingness to work). What is difficult is to predict their precise outcome and the time-lags involved. Such uncertainties are mainly the result of trying to manage demand in a mixed economy where two of its major components – private investment and exports minus imports – are inherently unknown to the authorities. The one depends so greatly on the *mood* of investors, and the other on largely external factors. Lastly, it has been shown time and again that it is one thing to get a policy working in the right direction to begin with, and quite another to reverse it when appropriate. It is by no means easy, when the time comes, to restore deflationary expectations to their former buoyancy.

To make matters worse, governments are far from sure about what they are aiming at – or even where they are starting from. A mass of economic data is certainly available to them, but much of it is either already out of date by the time it has been processed or subject to substantial margins of error. Predicting the future from such data is a hazardous business indeed. Sir Alec Cairncross, who was the government's chief economic advisor from 1964 to 1968, has subsequently written that he was 'amazed at the confidence with which precise forecasts were made' and never himself got beyond a 'rather impressionistic method of forecasting'.

Using only the very broad Keynesian instruments of management, we are therefore unlikely ever to achieve accurate stabilization of the economy. The techniques, given the intrinsic difficulties of economic forecasting in a mixed economy, are far too clumsy to do the job effectively.

(ii) Secondly, Keynes was naturally largely concerned with a single problem – that of finding a cure for the mass unemployment which was the plague of his times. Since the war, however, fortified by the increased understanding which Keynes brought about, we have become a great deal more ambitious. Governments have aimed at a *complex* of economic objectives: stabilization not only of a high-level employment but also of prices and the balance of payments – all in a context of rapid economic growth. What has been shown during these years is that they cannot all be simultaneously and consistently achieved by exclusive reliance on the broad macro-economic measures of the Keynesian package. Given the imprecision of those techniques, all sorts of policy conflicts can emerge. Full employment, for example, requires that the 'deflationary gap' be filled by further injections of demand. But suppose that too much demand is inadvertently pumped in? Then spending will be greater than that needed to purchase output at current prices, and prices will be pulled up in a demand-inflationary situation. Getting rid of the bulk of mass unemployment through Keynesian methods requires only their crude application. Balancing on the tightrope between less than full employment and excess demand is a very much more tasking exercise. Then again, the measures ordained by the achievement of one of the four immediate aims of economic policy may prove to be at odds with those dictated by another. It may be, for example, that weakness in the domestic economy (showing itself, amongst other ways, in rising unemployment) causes international selling pressure on the pound. To counter this the government might raise interest rates, hoping to persuade foreigners that pounds are still a worthwhile holding. But, while this may have the desired international effect, the impact on the domestic economy may be quite unwanted, intensifying the depression that already exists. Similar conflicts may also arise between any other pair of economic objectives.

(iii) Finally, the institutional framework of the economy is now radically different from that of Keynes's day. This, again, renders the techniques which he recommended for managing the economy less and less adequate. For example, unemployment with which he was concerned was essentially cyclical – caused by *demand* deficiency. That of the post war period, however, has partly been due to structural factors, and this, as we shall see in the next chapter, means that Keynesian remedies aren't appropriate. Similarly, the inflation of recent years has primarily stemmed from cost pressures rather than excess demand, and the Keynesian analysis and prescriptions are of dubious relevance in a context of giant corporations and highly organized labour power. The balance of payments and economic growth, too, are only to a limited degree susceptible to policies of demand manipulation – depending, as they do, more on underlying attitudes and institutions.

So much for basic theory – of the market mechanism, the Keynesian breakthrough and its major limitations. The next four chapters examine in more detail how far economic policy has been effective in achieving the often-stated objectives of full employment, price and balance of payments stability and faster economic growth. Subsequently, the objectives themselves will be called in question.

5

Jobs for Everyone

Most of the argument of the last few chapters has been concerned with the Keynesian conquest of mass unemployment, and with his demonstration that the level of employment and economic activity can be largely determined by government demand-management policies. And yet, in Britain during recent years, the number of people recorded as being jobless has sometimes hovered around the million mark. In the United States, under the administration of Mr Nixon (an avowed Keynesian!), the number of people out of work has often been closer to three million. And if we widen our perspective still further and recognize the plight of underdeveloped countries, we find that in India, for example, the problem of unemployment – either open or 'disguised' – is of quite staggering dimensions. What has gone wrong with Keynesianism?

To begin with the British case, the official unemployment statistics almost certainly understate the true extent of the problem. There are many people – particularly women – who would like jobs and can't find them, but who are not recorded as unemployed. Since they are not due for social security benefits and don't bother to register at labour exchanges in areas where there is patently no possibility of their getting work, their joblessness goes undetected. Nor do the statistics take into account young people who continue in full-time education simply because they know that they won't get jobs if they leave. And at the other end of the age-scale are elderly workers who 'voluntarily' retire prematurely because they have been made redundant and see no prospect of alternative employment. Finally, generally higher unemployment tends to be accompanied by short-time working and a reduction in overtime working which hits lower-paid workers (many of who depend on overtime earnings) particularly hard.[1]

Translating unemployment into percentage terms certainly makes the problem look rather less stark. At its worst, the number out of work in post-war years – when related to the total work-force – has never reached the 4 per cent level. However, the late sixties and early seventies saw a sharp deterioration in the situation, with unemployment three times the average level of the post-war period as a whole.

Moreover, unemployment does not affect all sections of the community equally. Amongst the youngest and oldest groups of workers, the percentage out of work is double that of the national average. General labourers and coloured workers are two categories particularly hard hit. The regional spread of unemployment, as we shall see later, is highly uneven. And a final indicator of the increasing *intensity* of unemployment is the lengthening period for which, on average, each worker remains without a job. Compounding these various elements – looking, for example, at the percentage of young or old manual workers unemployed in Northern Ireland or Scotland – highlights the fatuity of those who seek to minimize the problem by referring to the national average as '*only* 3–4%'. Unemployment today remains a matter of very serious concern.

But with this said, it is admittedly a problem of a quite different order from that of the thirties. Fig. 14 marks the contrast between unemployment averaging 14 per cent in the inter-war years and the dramatically lower post-war average.

However, we must still ask – if Keynes had really found the key to full employment – why has there been *any* unemployment in post-war Britain; and why, in particular, does the problem seem to have been getting worse rather than better? There are many elements in the explanation.

1. Some indication of the extent to which official statistics under-record actual unemployment is given in the Advance Analysis of the 1971 Census, which provisionally estimated that on Census day about 100,000 males and up to 700,000 females were seeking work or waiting to take up a job in April 1971 but were not registered as unemployed.

The Irreducible Minimum

There is, first of all, no prospect of achieving literally full employment in the sense that the whole of the work-force is constantly occupied. At any one time, people will be in the

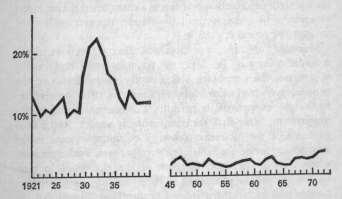

Figure 14. Unemployment 1921–72. (Source: The British Economy: Key Statistics 1900–1970, *London and Cambridge Economic Service, Dept of Employment and Productivity)*

process of moving from one job to another and these will show up in the figures as 'frictional' unemployment. The better the system of informing work-seekers of job opportunities, of bringing them into contact with potential employers, and the greater the advice and other financial help which is given to them, the lower will be the rate of frictional unemployment. Certainly, there are possibilities of improving the present network of labour exchanges and the information services which they offer.

Then again, another category which will always be with us are the unemployables – those who are too physically or mentally disabled to find work. This, unfortunately, is likely to be a growing group in an economy of increasing technological sophistication, as more and more people become unable to cope with the tensions or provide the skills needed in modern production techniques. Once again, the number can be minimized by policies deliberately aimed at creating special jobs using an appropriate technology, along the lines of a larger-scale 'Remploy', the government-sponsored agency which already provides employment for the handicapped.

Important though they are, neither frictional unemployment nor the unemployables represent more than a fraction of total unemployment, as can be seen from the fact that there *have* been post-war years with unemployment below 1 per cent.

Remnants of the Cycle

Since the outset of industrialization, modern capitalist economies have been plagued by periodic fluctuations commonly labelled the 'trade cycle'. Periods of booming economic activity – with employment at a high level, substantial investment and general prosperity – have been regularly followed by recessions deteriorating into more long-drawn-out slumps, marked by rising unemployment and depressed business expectations. This, in turn, gives way after a time to a gradual recovery phase, leading ultimately to a further boom.

The causes of fluctuations are broadly understood by economists, although the detailed mechanism remains a subject of debate. The trade cycle is essentially a product of the uncoordinated leakages and injections into the circular flow which we have already discussed. But that discussion was in static terms – to show the nature of equilibrium and disequilibrium. The trade cycle is a dynamic process of demand and output incompatibilities being regularly repeated in a pattern of ups and downs.

Take, for example, an initial slump situation transformed by an increase in total demand caused by an injection of investment. This, we know, will cause an even greater increase in income (via the multiplier). In turn, this may result in a further rise in investment – if investment is responsive to changes in the level of demand. What we have, then, is a process of cumulative expansion, and it is easy to see that any downward movement in income will similarly feed on itself. Quite what causes the upper and lower turning-points of the cycle is not so easy to explain. Booms, for example, may come to an end because of over-expansion of capacity or the existence of a full-employment ceiling or a revision of entrepreneurial expectations.

Whatever the particular explanation, the fact is that post-war fluctuations in economic activity have been within much narrower limits than in previous periods. The cycle is still with us, but in a much dampened form – and, what is more, it is based on an upward growth trend. That is to say, each recession is generally at a higher level of real income than the previous one; each boom reaches a higher peak than its predecessor. Fig. 15 illustrates the continued existence of the trade cycle and its reduced severity compared with earlier periods.

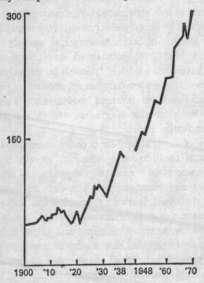

Figure 15. Industrial production. Base year 1924 = 100.

How far is the cycle due to the conscious manipulation of the level of total demand in the economy according to Keynesian principles? Paradoxically, one of the foremost students of economic policy in this period, J. C. R. Dow, has concluded that the overall effect of governmental measures has been 'positively destabilizing'. His argument follows from what we have already said: given faulty diagnosis and techniques that work imprecisely and with lengthy uncertain time-lags, stimulatory policies tend to bite at the wrong time – just when private consumption and investment are beginning to pick up. And similarly on the downward leg of the cycle there is also a tendency to overshoot.

However, even given this unfortunate possibility that economic imbalances are frequently over-corrected by government policies, it probably remains true that the relative mildness of post-war cycles is at least partly attributable to increased economic understanding and demand stabilization measures. The level at which the cycle continues to operate is a very much higher one than in previous periods, and the danger of it becoming cumulatively out of hand has largely been eradicated.

On the other hand, there is evidence that the vestige which remains of the 'natural' business cycle has been accentuated by the superimposition of a new 'political' – or, more frankly, 'electoral' – cycle. A government going to the country naturally wishes to do so in the most auspicious circumstances. The past tends to be forgotten, and if it can show a picture of immediate prosperity – a rapid rate of economic growth, near-full employment, a strong balance of payments and reasonable price stability – it is likely to do well.

The existence of such desiderata is no longer entirely beyond the control of a government. To some extent they can be deliberately planned for. The need to 'get the economy right' at the appropriate political moment is only one factor making demand stabilization difficult. (The balance of payments, the subject of Chapter 7, is obviously another.) Both have certainly contributed to the tedious pattern of 'stop–go' to which we have become so accustomed.

The chances are that a newly-elected government will inherit an economy booming dangerously to the point at which there are pressures overspilling into increased demand for imports, causing balance of payments difficulties and rising prices at home. The new administration boldly faces up to the situation as it finds it, and applies the necessary discipline in the knowledge that it will not have to face the electorate again for another five years. This is the 'stop' period – one of monetary restraint, deflationary fiscal policy in the form of higher taxes and budget surpluses, and a dampening down of the expectations of the private sector. Unemployment rises, the increase in national income is either halted or even marginally reversed, the exchange rate may be adjusted – and the scene is set for a new advance. We are now into the third year, perhaps, of the new administration, which, having taken a series of measures unpopular but necessary in the national interest, begins to focus its attention on the next election. It is time for expansion. Credit becomes easier, the electoral promise to reduce taxes is finally fulfilled, export demand (as a result of the exchange-rate adjustment) offers a further stimulus. Hopefully, the economy moves onto an upward path again. The timing is delicate. Private investment, in particular, having been deliberately depressed during the 'stop' phase, may prove awkwardly obstinate in responding to the new favourable climate which the government has aimed to create. The danger, at this point, is that the authorities react by pumping in still more demand. The result is that trouble is stored up for the future. Whether it is for them – as the newly re-elected government – or for their unfortunate successors is a matter which there is still insufficient expertise or control to precisely determine.

This is a greatly simplified and perhaps over-cynical representation of what actually happens. There is nonetheless something in it. Governments may not, perhaps, pursue a strategy over their five-year term quite so Machiavellian as has been indicated here. They will almost certainly see themselves as reacting to the needs of the current situation in an appropriately responsible matter. But Fig. 16 suggests that the political element has now become deeply built into the trade cycle – or that the cycle itself has been modified to fit in with the idiosyncrasies of the British electoral system. There is a remarkable coincidence between election years and more rapid increases in earnings and gross national product.

Whatever the cause, the fact is that the economy is still subject to cyclical fluctuations, and that part of the recurring unemployment problem is therefore of the traditional 'Keynesian' variety. It is caused by inadequate total demand and is therefore in principle soluble by the basic Keynesian techniques of demand injection through monetary and fiscal measures.

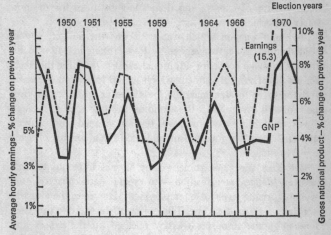

Figure 16. The trade cycle.

It is interesting to try to determine the extent to which current demand-deficiency unemployment is the unwanted product of imprecise diagnostic and remedial techniques, and how far it is an element in deliberate government policy. Is it simply that we lack the know-how and weapons to cope with marginal rather than mass unemployment of the Keynesian type? Or have governments learned the Keynesian lesson so well that they now apply his methods deliberately to *create* additional unemployment? We must focus on the history of the years following 1967 to find an answer to this disturbing question.

In November 1967, the Labour government, having for three years defended the sanctity of the exchange rate even more zealously than its Conservative predecessors, finally bowed to the wind and devalued the pound by 14 per cent. This done, it had to take measures to make devaluation work. Devaluation simply meant that our exports tended to become cheaper, and imports into this country more expensive. But if the balance of payments was to improve as a result of these changes in relative prices, there had to be sufficient productive capacity in British industry to take advantage of the situation – to provide an additional volume of exports and domestic substitutes for the now dearer imports.

The main weapon which was used was the budget, seldom wielded quite so aggressively as by Roy Jenkins in 1968. In his attempt to make room for additional exports (and for the likely increase in private investment which would follow on increased profitability in foreign markets), he aimed at withdrawing over £900 million a year from the economy through increased taxes. Moreover, public expenditure was severely pruned, and between 1967 and 1970 the government budgeted for a surplus of some £2,700 million.

Here, then, was a government using Keynesian techniques in a massively *deflationary* fashion – to create spare capacity, and, inevitably, rising levels of unemployment. However, the aim was essentially a short-term one. The object of the exercise was then to *redeploy* the resources thereby released, in the export and investment sectors of the economy. It represented a once and for all switch in the employment pattern to achieve the sort of expansion which had generally evaded governments in the past – expansion led from export and investment demand rather than the more common upsurge in consumer spending. This, it was hoped, would at long last set the economy on the virtuous path of non-inflationary growth.

It was not to be. Resources proved much more difficult to redeploy than they had been to 'shake out'. The time-lags involved in achieving the benefits of devaluation were considerable. As it became clear that the economy was hardly going to be looking its best for the coming election, the Labour government in its last year of office largely abandoned any remaining hold which it had on incomes and prices. The newly elected Conservative government, when it took office in 1970, was faced with a more rapidly rising price level than at any other period during the post-war years.

In this situation, it was disinclined to expand the economy. On the contrary, it continued in the first place to exert still further *deflationary* pressure, presumably hoping that the resulting increase in unemployment might dampen the inflationary fires, either by eliminating any possibility of excess demand in the economy, or simply by reducing trade-union militancy. Only when this policy was decisively shown to be ineffective (for reasons which will be discussed in the following chapter) did the government finally make a belated attempt to reflate the economy.

Thus it can be argued that part of the unemployment of the late sixties and early seventies was certainly of the Keynesian 'demand-deficiency' type. Partly it was due to the imprecisions of demand management which we have already noted. But to some extent it was also a product of deliberate policy on the part of the two governments: firstly to create the excess capacity necessary to make devaluation work, and secondly as an anti-inflationary device.

Regional Disparities

We have already questioned how far the official statistics fully reflect the true extent of unemployment. We have also seen that joblessness is concentrated in particular age and occupational groups. The figures can also be disaggregated to reveal dramatic differences in the geographical spread of unemployment between the various parts of the country (Table 2).

Table 2: Unemployment (registered) percentage

	1968	1969	1970	1971
U.K.	2·5	2·5	2·7	3·7
North	4·7	4·8	4·8	5·9
Yorkshire and Humberside	2·6	2·6	2·9	4·0
East Midlands	1·9	2·0	2·3	3·1
East Anglia	2·0	1·9	2·1	3·1
South-East	1·6	1·6	1·7	2·0
South-West	2·5	2·7	2·8	3·4
West Midlands	2·2	2·0	2·3	4·0
North-West	2·5	2·5	2·8	4·1
Wales	4·0	4·1	4·0	4·7
Scotland	3·8	3·7	4·3	6·0
North Ireland	7·2	7·3	7·0	8·0

What emerges from Table 2 is that, when judged by unemployment (and other indicators, like income, roughly follow suit),

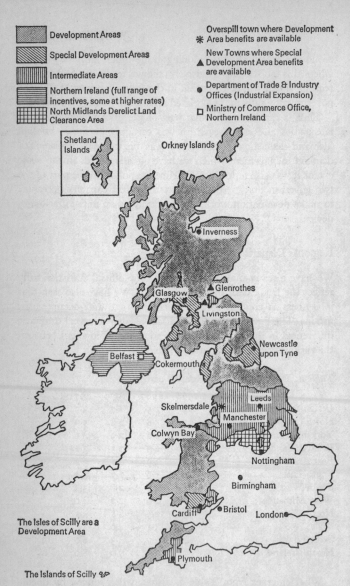

Figure 17. The assisted areas. (*Source: Dept of Trade and Industry*)

Britain suffers from acute regional imbalance. Moreover, the problem is not one of isolated islands of relative depression in a sea of general prosperity. On the contrary, the relatively poorer regions happen to comprise the greater part of the country outside a belt of high employment stretching through the South-East to the Midlands. This is illustrated in Fig. 17, in which only the unshaded areas are deemed not to require official regional assistance of one kind or another. No less than 44 per cent of the population live in 'assisted areas'.

The genesis of the regional problem – which has been with us for a long time – lies essentially in the loosening of ties which traditionally dictated the location of various industries. No longer do industries need to be sited beside fast-moving rivers or on the coalfields; the development of modern sources of power has greatly widened their possible location choices. Nor is proximity to the source of raw materials a vital consideration for the majority of firms.

In these circumstances, locational pulls tend to be towards the *market*, with firms establishing themselves in areas combining a high level of prosperity and population density. And, secondly, liberation from traditional locational influences means that the existence of 'external economies' now plays an increasingly important part in deciding where a new plant should be sited.

External economies are the benefits which the individual firm derives from working near a group of other successful firms. To choose such an area means, for example, that workers will be available who are used to working in that particular industry, and that the training facilities in the area such as those provided in the local technical colleges will be geared to the industry's needs. The transport and communications network, power services, housing and other social amenities will all tend to reflect the requirements of the industrial complex and the general prosperity of the area. The existence of a basic industrial concentration will attract ancillary firms, firms which use what would otherwise be waste products as the raw material for their own production, firms which produce components for the main industries. And, finally, working near enterprises in a similar line of business enables a firm to keep in touch with what is going on –

to be aware of technical changes, new markets, new products.

These, then, are the advantages of concentration. Success attracts those anxious to share in the benefits, and it is easy to see that, once an initial disparity between regions has been established, the gap between them will tend to widen. Fig. 18 gives a stylized explanation of the widening disparity between 'London' and 'Scotland'.

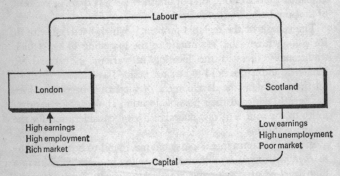

Figure 18

As can be seen, both capital and labour move from Scotland to London. Capital flows in response to the forces which have just been described. Labour is on the move looking for work and higher earnings. And the workers which migrate are most likely to be the young, those with initiative, those who think they have skills to offer. The overall effect is to make Scotland even less attractive to firms than it was in the first place. Stage by stage, London becomes cumulatively more attractive and Scotland less so.

All of this is contrary to what might be expected from a simple market economy. According to the theory, low-wage or unemployed labour from Scotland would certainly tend to move southwards. But would there not be counter-attractions for *capital* in Scotland – cheap labour, cheap housing, under-utilized social amenities, lack of congestion on the London scale?

The problem in the real world is, of course, that labour in an area of declining industries will have the wrong skills and, sometimes, a history of embittered industrial relations; the social capital – housing, schools, hospitals – are likely to be of poor quality; the transport system will have been built to serve a quite different pattern of production; and wages, when negotiated on a national basis, may turn out to be no lower.

All in all, left to its own devices, the market system has powerful centripetal tendencies. That is why governments, concerned about the social and economic consequences of major regional disparities, have intervened since way back in the thirties to try to bring about more even balance. Over the years, the basic policy mix has been the same: a combination of deterrents to further location in the more prosperous regions and inducements to firms to site new plans elsewhere. What has changed, time after time, is the scale of regional policy, its coverage (which areas should be included?) and the specific sticks and carrots.

The results of forty years of regional policy are rather disappointing. Hard-core regional unemployment persists, accentuated periodically by the relatively greater sensitivity of the regions to general deflation of the economy. Policy over these years has suffered from perhaps five major defects.

(i) For much of the period, assistance to the regions was seen more as a form of charity relief than as a positive contribution towards the growth of the economy as a whole. Once it is recognized that to solve the 'Scottish' problem is simultaneously to relieve the 'London' problem of over-congestion, once the growth potential of the assisted areas is fully understood, then regional balance can be viewed as *economically* beneficial as well as socially desirable.

(ii) The enormous number of changes in the detailed approach of successive governments has created an aura of uncertainty which is itself a further disincentive to firms to establish themselves in the relatively poorer two-thirds of the country. Fears, for example, that an area may be due for demotion in the scale of development assistance, or that particular inducements like the regional-employment premium may be phased out, hardly create a satisfactory basis for confident long-term investment.

(iii) Policies have concentrated rather narrowly on job creation through the encouragement of manufacturing industry and have neglected other, more labour-intensive activities – service industries, the re-location of company head offices and government administrative and research establishments.

(iv) There has also been too little emphasis on the retraining of workers in the assisted regions and on encouraging movement of workers within the regions. Retraining has to be in appropriate skills related to job opportunities, and in both this qualitative aspect and in the scale of our industrial retraining programmes Britain appears decidedly backward compared with other countries. A recent study by Mukherjee, for example, shows that, allowing for the difference in the size of its working force, Britain would have had to spend some £317 million on retraining to have kept up with the recent Swedish increase in spending on such programmes.[2]

(v) We have still not come to grips with the scale of the regional problem. The sum just mentioned for one part of a comprehensive policy in fact exceeds the *total* spending on all aspects of regional policy, despite a very substantial increase which took place during the sixties.

How effective, then, has regional policy been? The most recent and comprehensive attempt at evaluation is that of John Rhodes and Barry Moore of the Department of Applied Economics at Cambridge University.[3] The conclusion that they come to from their studies is that policies have broadly prevented the regional problem from getting worse. For example, they estimate that the measures of the 1960s diverted nearly a quarter of a million jobs to the assisted areas. But to have eliminated regional unemployment, some 800–900,000 new jobs would have been needed. At recent rates of progress it would take about forty years to get rid of present regional employment disparities.

The answer does not lie in more active Keynesianism. Increasing the level of demand in the economy means that the prosperous regions inevitably hit full employment before the others. Further increases in demand merely create inflationary

2. S. Mukherjee, *Making Labour Markets Work*, P.E.P. Broadsheet 532, p. 12.
3. B. Moore and J. Rhodes, 'Evaluating the Effects of British Regional Policy', *Economic Journal*, March 1973.

pressures. And, on top of that, there is no way in which increased demand can be contained within a poorer region. It is bound to overspill into the rest of the economy.

Keynesianism fails to solve the problem of regional unemployment because its cause is not demand-deficiency. It is due to an inadequate inducement to invest in the poorer regions because of their inappropriately skilled work-force and often inadequate infrastructure, coupled with the positive attractions of the richer 'south'. In other words, it is a matter of 'supply-deficiency' rather than demand-deficiency – unemployment more akin to that which plagues underdeveloped countries.

If we are concerned to narrow the gap between poorer and richer regions – either because it is politically expedient to do so or because it economically pays or because it is regarded as simply humanly intolerable that people's economic prospect should be so affected by the chance of where they happen to be born in this small country – clearly still more positive policies must be devised. Partly this is a matter of recognizing the dimensions of the problem and spending accordingly large sums in solving it. And partly it is a matter of searching for new approaches and techniques. The answer may lie in giving regional authorities more financial autonomy in the hope that *they* will have the initiative to sell themselves more successfully. Or more specific intervention from the centre may be called for, amounting, in effect, to *direction* of firms to development areas.

British entry into Europe both highlights and complicates the regional issue. Within Britain, the effect of joining the Common Market will be that the forces making for concentration in London and the South-east will be further strengthened. And the process of cumulative causation which we have already described working within this country will also work *between* countries of the enlarged Community as well. The likelihood that prosperity will be concentrated in the so-called 'golden triangle' bounded by Birmingham, Düsseldorf and Milan is graphically illustrated in Fig. 19.

The danger of Britain becoming the 'poor man of Europe' is a real one unless Community policies with regard to regional balance can be transformed from their current limited concern

Figure 19. The likely assisted areas of the enlarged E.E.C. (The Financial Times, *30 November 1972*)

with alleviating the effects of agricultural change to a recognition, backed by vigorous policy measures, of the need for the fruits of economic progress to be fairly shared between partners.

Finally, there is an element of unemployment which arises from the continuing substitution of capital for labour, the introduction of machines to do what once was done by workers. By and large, technological progress is to be welcomed because it reduces the necessity of physical hard work and the drudgery of labour. More output from less effort offers the possibility of increased leisure and greater material wellbeing.

But part of our present unemployment, and part of the explanation of extreme wage differentials, arise from the fact that the benefits of increased mechanization have not so far been evenly spread amongst the working community. The danger of which we have to beware is that, once again as in underdeveloped countries, our development becomes 'dualistic' – with a highly modern and prosperous industrial sector living in uneasy co-existence with a relatively impoverished, high-unemployment, traditional sector. This is a matter which we shall return to in Chapter 9.

Achieving full employment thus takes us well beyond simple Keynesian demand-management techniques. It is a multidimensional problem which involves influences on the supply side too, and ensuring a fair spread of employment opportunities. Above all, it is the human aspect which must be stressed. A fast rate of economic growth, a high level of national material prosperity – these will mean little unless their benefits can be dispersed. The consequences of a low priority for employment in the hierarchy of national objectives are there for all to see – in the sickness of American society, and, closer to home, in Northern Ireland. It is no coincidence that in Londonderry, before the troubles, the rate of joblessness amongst males was over 14 per cent.

6

The Inflation Bogey

We have suffered from inflation throughout the whole of the post-war period and in the nineteen-seventies it has emerged as the main problem exercising the authorities' attention. For ordinary people, too, failure to achieve price stability is the defect of the economy of which they are most aware. Certainly they are concerned about unemployment, but that, as we have seen, happens to be unevenly dispersed and does not affect the great majority; the balance of payments, although the politicians may have succeeded in inculcating a sense of national guilt about our inability to pay our international way, remains a remote abstraction from everyday life; even the rate of economic growth is not a matter of direct significance to people who, after all, do not always see it reflected in their own standard of living. But rising prices are something which affect us all – something of which we have immediate everyday experience. And yet we vainly elect one government after another on the basis of their promise to stabilize prices only to find that their particular panacea turns out to be as illusory as that of their predecessors.

Perhaps we have our priorities wrong. Perhaps inflation is not so much of a problem as it seems. For one thing, we should count ourselves lucky not to have been born, for example, Indonesian. In 1966, that unfortunate economy suffered price rises averaging 60 per cent per *month*. In British terms, that would mean that a pound at the beginning of October would be worth only 62½ pence by November – inflation at the rate of over 1,000 per cent per annum. Unfortunately, tales such as this, far from reassuring people that our own inflation is comparatively mild, merely show the ultimate disaster (of runaway, or hyper-inflation) for which, they fear, we are already heading.

It is important to put the British inflation into perspective. Firstly, rising prices have, after all, been with us now for a very long time – to be precise, since 1934 (and the preceding period, in which prices were actually falling, was not a memorably happy economic episode, accompanied, as it was, by mass unemployment, extreme business fluctuations and industrial unrest). Moreover, the rate of inflation has not been getting *consistently* worse. Periods of rather sharply rising prices have been followed by years of more moderate price increases (Fig. 20). But the popular impression of a sharp recent deterioration

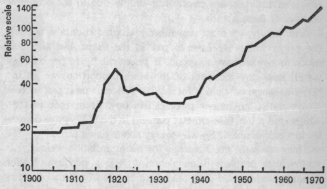

Figure 20. The retail price index 1900–1970. (Source: The British Economy: Key Statistics 1900–1970, *London and Cambridge Economic Service, Table E.)*

is correct: the seventies have seen a more rapid rate of inflation than anything previously experienced since the war.

It is easy, too, to adopt an insular view of inflation – to fall for the notion that it is a peculiarly British problem stemming from some deep-seated malaise from which so many commentators have gloomily assured us that we are suffering. It is nothing of the sort. Inflation in the recent past has been a world-wide phenomenon, except in the communist bloc, which has experienced, apart from Yugoslavia, near-zero inflation. All other economies have more or less suffered from price rises – and the broad division between the 'more or less' is an interesting one. A recent study shows that countries are divided into two quite distinct clusters. There are those in which inflation has been less than 10 per cent per annum, and there are those suffering 'strato-inflation' where price rises are regularly of the order of 20 to 35 per cent annually. Oddly, no countries fall into the intermediate category of between 10 and 20 per cent.[1]

Strato-inflation is largely confined to underdeveloped economies. Within the group of advanced industrial nations with inflation less than 10 per cent per annum, Britain's record on prices has been worse than many but better than others. The causes of inflation are clearly not simply due to the economic oddities of these islands.

And, finally, we must remember that what counts is not just the prices which we have to pay in the shops, but also how much money we have to spend. If prices rise by 10 per cent but we all have pay increases of the same proportion, we are no better or worse off than before. What concerns us is *real* income – how much our money incomes can buy. From 1960 to 1970 while retail prices rose some 45 per cent in the U.K., gross domestic incomes doubled. So why worry about rising prices?

There *are* some good reasons for taking inflation seriously. It is, firstly, a problem if people *think* it is a problem. If, for example, savings and investment are deterred by fears of growing inflation, such lack of confidence in the prospects for the economy will adversely affect the prospects for the economy (although there is no evidence that this has happened over any length of time). Then again, if we start building into wage and price increases expectations of increasing inflation in the future, this will result in more rapid inflation in the future. But so long as we are able to adjust to any given inflationary rate, should rising prices be a matter for concern?

The need to maintain Britain's international competitiveness is another common argument put forward to support attempts to control inflation. If British manufacturing prices get out of line, it becomes more difficult for us to sell exports, and easier

1. D. Jackson and H. A. Turner, 'Inflation, Strato-inflation and Social Conflict', in *Do Trade Unions Cause Inflation?*, University of Cambridge Department of Applied Economics Occasional Paper 36, 1972.

for foreigners to penetrate British markets. The consequent balance of payments difficulties make it necessary for governments to resort to painful remedies like domestic deflation. Inflation can thus result in higher unemployment and slower economic growth. Even here, however, the case is not that we should achieve total price stability, but merely that our own rate of inflation should not greatly differ from the average which our main international competitors are experiencing. To some extent it is possible to offset the international consequences of an above-average inflation rate by adjustments to the external exchange rate such as the devaluation of 1967 or the floating of the pound in 1972. But it should be remembered, firstly, that full membership of the E.E.C. may ultimately involve loss of independence in determining the rate at which the pound should exchange for other currencies. And secondly, as will be seen, devaluation can itself give a further twist to the inflationary spiral, require a shift of resources from the domestic market to exports, and sometimes involve a temporary decline in real living standards. So, from this point of view, inflation in excess of that of our competitors *does* create real difficulties.

But what above all makes inflation a problem to be reckoned with are its effects on the distributive share-out of national income. It does not affect us all equally. The incomes of firms and shareholders, for example, are fairly closely tied to the price level; management are broadly in a position to fix their own salaries, ensuring that they keep up with current price increases; for many professional people and white-collared workers, annual seniority increments provide an immediate cushion against price rises; highly organized workers have the bargaining strength to prevent *their* real incomes from being eroded by inflation. The real burden of inflation falls on those whose incomes are relatively fixed – either because of their weak bargaining position or because they are particularly susceptible to administrative restraint. Their ranks may include creditors and rentiers, but it is also the low-paid, the pensioners and public-sector employees who are commonly hardest hit. The redistributive effects of inflation are unfortunately arbitrary.

Inflation is a problem, then, principally because of its

deleterious side-effects. If more attention was paid to offsetting these by specific policy measures, rising prices need not, perhaps, cause the dismay which they do – except, of course, if inflation shows signs of getting out of hand and becoming cumulative. But since we have not succeeded in preventing the unwanted distortions of the inflationary process, how should we set about achieving, if not complete price stability, at least less rapid price increases and keeping inflation within acceptably moderate and fairly predictable annual limits? What in fact are the causes of the current inflationary pressures? Economists, alas, are in no position to give a simple, straightforward answer.

We shall look to begin with at three types of explanation – those which see inflation as an essentially *monetary* phenomenom, those which emphasize excess demand as the main *pull* on prices, and those which identify cost *push* as the villain.

Too Much Money?

This was perhaps once the most popular of the man-in-the-street analyses of inflation – that it was all a matter of 'too much money chasing too few goods'. Rising prices were the result of failure on the part of governments to limit their recourse to the printing presses. It was a view which for a very long time also commanded the general support of economists. Pre-Keynesian thinking suggested that the level of economic activity, employment and real wages were all determined by factors such as thriftiness and productivity. Money was a 'veil' drawn over the real economic situation; all that money determined was the general price level.

The 'Quantity Theory' of money stated a simple causal relationship. For any given level of national output, the greater the amount of money in circulation the higher would be the price level at which transactions took place. The answer to inflation therefore lay in checking the money supply and limiting its increase to the rate at which the economy was growing. The Keynesian revolution, with its emphasis on spending rather than money supply as the main strategic variable, seemed to have dealt the Quantity Theory a fatal blow. But in recent years it has been resurrected, primarily as the result of the work of Professor Milton Friedman and the Chicago School of economists.

What their work shows is that over a long period of time the correlation between money supply and the level of economic activity has, for industrial economies, been an extremely close one. On the basis of this statistical relationship, the new monetarists argue that tightly disciplined control of the money supply stands a far better chance of achieving economic stabilization than all the 'meddling' of Keynesian techniques.

However, to show that historically changes in the money supply have been closely accompanied by corresponding changes in the level of economic activity does not in itself tell us anything about the causal relationships between the two. To throw some light on the matter, we will borrow the analogy used by Professor Kaldor in a recent attack on the monetarist position.[2]

Every Christmas, Kaldor points out, the British public sharply increase their spending. And every Christmas, if you look at the figures, you will find that the amount of banknotes in circulation also substantially rises. Should we conclude from this that it is the expansion of the supply of banknotes which *causes* the increased spending by the public? It would be a very foolish conclusion to come to because the real facts of the matter are well known.

We spend more because Christmas, in our particular culture, happens to be a time of unparalleled extravagance and general benevolence. The note supply is deliberately increased by the authorities because our greater spending *requires* more notes to service it. It is not the larger note circulation which causes our wild spending at Christmas; it is the other way round. And each January, as spending by the public dies down again, the monetary authorities withdraw an appropriate quantity of notes from circulation.

Supposing, however, that one year a Scrooge administration tried to curb our excesses by refusing to make the customary expansion in the December note supply. Would it succeed? Of course not. What would happen initially is that customers going to their banks to withdraw cash would be told by the banks,

2. N. Kaldor, 'The New Monetarism', *Lloyds Bank Review*, July 1970.

'Sorry, we've temporarily run out. Please come back later.' However, traumatic incidents like these would not deter would-be spenders. Out would come their various credit cards. They would also find that, in the circumstances, the shops would be only too anxious to offer credit themselves. And meanwhile the banks would be doing their bit to ease the situation by urging traders to bank their takings several times a day. In other words, we should overcome the scarcity of banknotes by making the limited stock *work* harder, turn over more rapidly. In economists' parlance, limitation in the supply of money will be offset by an increase in its 'velocity of circulation'.

The financial flexibility of a modern economy is such that it is possible to accommodate pretty well *any* level of spending to a given money supply. It even proved possible to overcome the extreme inconvenience caused by the Irish bank strike of 1970 when, for six months, the supply of banknotes and credit was completely cut off.

What is left of the monetarist case? Well, they argue, it may be that technically it is possible for the velocity of circulation of money to vary within wide limits. But, in fact, it has remained historically extremely stable. However, as Professor Kaldor argues, this is probably precisely because the monetarist prescriptions have not been heeded by governments. Since the authorities have in the past by and large passively adjusted the money supply to the level of spending, it has not been necessary for the velocity of circulation to alter. But if they did ever try to regulate spending via limitation of the money stock, then we would soon find ways round the attempted discipline.

Those, in short, are the basic pros and cons of the debate on the importance of the money supply in achieving price stability. It is a continuing controversy from which no dogmatic conclusions can be drawn. The odds, however, certainly seem against those who believe that monetary restraint can alone do the anti-inflationary trick – particularly while as yet they have failed to offer any satisfactory account of the precise mechanism by which a greater quantity of money becomes translated into higher prices.

Too Much Spending?

The Keynesian view of inflation, which appeared to have super-seded the Quantity Theory, stresses the role of spending as a threat to price stability. Changes in the money supply fail to explain inflation precisely because increases in the amount of money need *not* be spent. They can be, and are, partly held in the form of 'idle balances'. People and firms hold money balances for a variety of reasons – to finance expected trans-actions, against a rainy day, and in order to take advantage of opportunities as they arise in the future.

For Keynesians, it is the flow of expenditure – on consump-tion, on investment and on exports, by individuals, firms and foreigners – in relation to the flow of output which determines what happens to the general price level. Keynes himself was, of course, mostly concerned about the situation in which spending plans fell short of the level needed to absorb full-capacity out-put. The consequent 'deflationary gap' was the source of the mass unemployment which was the greatest problem of his time. But the analysis can also be applied to the opposite situation – that in which the various plans to spend add up to a total in excess of the value of full employment output measured at cur-rent prices. This is the problem of the 'inflationary gap', with total demand in the economy exceeding total supply. When there is large-scale unemployment in the economy, the effect of demand exceeding supply is to bring idle resources into employ-ment again. The temporary excess of demand over supply means that retailers run short of stocks and increase their orders to the manufacturers. Provided that they are working in a competitive market, the manufacturers' response is not to in-crease prices, but to take on more workers and expand output. The increased demand *can* soon be met by an increased supply of goods and services so that there is no *need* for prices to alter. But at full employment (or indeed as full employment is approached), any excess demand in the economy can only show itself in the form of higher prices. As we try to spend our in-creased incomes, since there are no more goods and services available, all that will happen is that the prices which we pay are pulled up by our increased expenditure.

Demand-pull inflation is a very likely condition in mixed economies accepting a wide range of social responsibilities and practising Keynesian stabilization techniques. Partly it is a matter of trying to do too much. The government wants resources for its welfare programmes, for defence spending, for education and the rest. At the same time it is stimulating the private sector to undertake more investment to modernize and expand production. Consumers are constantly bidding to increase their material standards of living. These competing demands may easily exceed the output which can be produced from available resources. But how can they be trimmed down? Partly the problem is one of priorities – with governments reluctant to reduce this or that particularly pressing programme of expenditure; too much is finally left in, with the hope that the rate of economic growth will somehow prove sufficient to accommodate the lot. Partly it is a matter of not really knowing what, for example, private investment or exports are actually going to amount to. And partly, as we have already seen, the problem is that governments lack the techniques to 'finely tune' the economy to just the right level.

Together, these difficulties mean that excess-demand inflation is a very real threat and there is little doubt that at many times during the post-war years it is this variety of inflation from which the British economy has primarily suffered.

The search for a solution led to the development of a body of economic thinking during the sixties to a conclusion which was distinctly unpalatable. Professor Frank Paish, for example, argued that the real cure to demand inflation was the creation of more spare capacity in the economy. Since prices began to rise before full employment was reached and since, anyway, stabilization techniques were far too crude to keep the economy at just the full-employment level, the answer was to work with sufficient unemployment to both eliminate excess demand and leave room for the possibility of 'overshooting'.

However, before considering the more detailed policy implication of the Paishite thesis, we should first look at a third explanation of inflation – that which sees the pressure of costs as the main element in rising prices.

Costs and Prices

Cost-push theorists need not deny the possibility of excess-demand inflation. What they do argue is that, even when demand is quite evidently not excessive, inflation can still come about independently through pressures operating on the supply side. When firms' prices generally are composed of costs plus an appropriate mark-up for profits, rising costs will soon be reflected in rising prices regardless of the state of overall demand – as businesses struggle to maintain their profit margins.

This approach is probably now the most popular of the various explanations of the inflationary process. For which element in costs has risen most persistently and relentlessly over the years? The real culprit, it is argued, is exorbitant wage increases. When wage rates increase by over 17 per cent, as they did, for example, between October 1971 and October 1972, need one look any further for the causes of current inflation? Here, then, is the spectre of organized labour so powerful as to hold the country to ransom. An academic pointer to the way in which wage-inflation might be dealt with came from the historical researches of Professor A. W. Phillips, which suggested that there had been a long-term relationship in the United Kingdom between the percentage of unemployment and the annual rate of wage-rate change.[3] The higher the percentage unemployed, the lower the rate at which wages increased. There was a clear 'trade-off' between employment and price stability, which meant that society would have to face up to a decidedly awkward choice about priorities (Fig. 21).

The Phillips curve was first found to hold good for the period 1861–1913. But, remarkably, further work showed that the relationship between unemployment and wage-rate changes remained fairly stable during the radically different conditions

3. A. W. Phillips, 'The Relation between Unemployment and the Rate of Change of Money Wage Rates in the United Kingdom, 1861–1957', *Economica*, November, 1958.

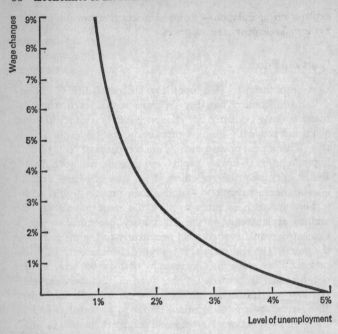

Figure 21. A Phillips curve

which prevailed during the inter-war years and the post-war period up to the mid-sixties. It looked very much as though it could serve both as a predictive tool for forecasting future changes, and also as a basis on which painful policy decisions would have to be taken.

In this latter respect, the Paishite line of argument and the Phillips relationship both signposted the same course of action. Doubt about whether the country was suffering from demand-pull or cost-push inflation could be relegated to quarrelsome academics, because both sorts of inflation called for the same solution. If price stability was the main policy priority, it could be achieved only by modifying what had hitherto been regarded as the most sacrosanct of objectives – full employment. Deliberately created unemployment – only, it was argued, of relatively minor proportions – would kill both birds with one stone. On the one hand, it would strike directly at the roots of any excess demand in the economy. On the other, by reducing trade-union militancy or whatever other causal process was hidden behind the Phillips curve, *cost*-inflation would at the same time be brought under control.

One of the great laments of those economists who aspire to be real scientists is their inability to manipulate economic forces in laboratory conditions in the way that their counterparts in physics and chemistry are able to do. But, as luck would have it, they were actually given the opportunity – in the late sixties and early seventies – to see an experiment. Unemployment, for reasons we have already discussed, *was* allowed by the government to increase. The Phillips hypothesis suggested that the result would be a dampening down of the rate of wage increases; and this, in turn, should have meant a reduction in the rate of inflation.

Unfortunately, the Great Experiment failed. Mysteriously, as unemployment increased so also did the wage rates. Far from achieving price stability, higher unemployment than at any time since the war was accompanied by an unprecedented rate of inflation. British governments created what had hitherto been achieved only in the United States – a combination of a stagnant economy, high unemployment and rampant prices. It was a result which was not only undesirable, but one which should, according to economists, have been impossible. What went wrong?

To some extent, the breakdown of the Phillips relationship can be attributed to the policy of labour 'shake-out' encouraged in the late sixties by the Selective Employment Tax. This may have reversed employers' strategy in previous recessions of 'hoarding' labour in the hope of a quick upturn in economic activity. But what still has to be explained is the failure of increased unemployment to reduce trade-union bargaining strength. Higher unemployment has led to more rather than less militancy. There are a number of reasons why this was so.

(i) First of all, it must be recognized that there have been a range of other cost-push pressures affecting the price level quite independently of wages. Two of the most important are the rise in import prices resulting from the 1967 devaluation and the 1972 'float'; and the increase in unit costs of manufacturing industry arising from working with excess capacity. Producers have thus had a double reason for raising prices quite apart from increased wage costs. They have been paying more for their raw materials; and, in a severe recession, they have had to spread their overheads over reduced output; that is, deflationary policies, by lowering the level of plant utilization, are themselves a cost-inflationary pressure.

Workers have therefore been faced with both higher food prices and rising prices of manufactured goods due to factors other than their own actions. To this extent, wage claims are defensive reaction on the part of the unions rather than the prime movers in creating cost inflation.

(ii) Other government policies have also played their part in accelerating inflation. 'Fair' rents, increased charges for school meals and the changes in personal and profits taxation introduced by the Conservative government on its election in 1970 all represented a redistribution of national income in favour of higher-income groups. Again, substantial wage claims could naturally be expected as workers tried to avoid an erosion in their real standard of living. Moreover, the anticipated effects of higher food prices and the change-over to V.A.T. which would result from entry into Europe may have contributed to strengthening expectations of still faster inflation in the future.

(iii) Finally, the fact that the worst inflation coincided with a period of economic stagnation is no accident. In the context of post-war economic growth, we have become accustomed to expect that, year by year, our real standard of living will increase. Politicians promise that it will be so – and for most of us, by and large, it has proved true. When the economy moves into recession, these expectations are not automatically choked off. But if the economy is not growing, if there is no increase taking place in the amount of goods and services produced, then how can any of us be better off? The answer is, of course, that we can only do so at the expense of others. If some groups are successful in securing higher real incomes, then it must mean that other groups have become worse off. We are always interested in questions of distribution – about how we stand in relation to others. But in a no-growth situation – when the national cake remains the same size – relative shares are all that we have to squabble about.

These are muddy waters. There is no simple cause of inflation. It is facile to conclude from the wage-price spiral that it must be wage increases which lie at the root of the problem. We must ask *why* wages are increasing. Inflation, as we have seen, *can* arise from quite different sources – from trying as an economy to do more than we have the resources available for, from independent pressures on prices quite distinct from wage-push and from the effects of government policies themselves. Above all, it must be clear that inflation is more than a merely technical economic process. What lie behind it are questions of social justice and equity, of struggles between different groups in the economy to secure more favourable positions. To some extent inflation, by blurring the distinction between money and real income and by allowing temporary readjustments in relative income positions, acts as an escape valve to these underlying social pressures. Solving the inflationary problem therefore means facing up to these fundamental distributional issues. This is a matter to which we shall return in later chapters.

Postscript. 1973–4 saw a marked acceleration in the rate of inflation in the United Kingdom and other industrial economies chiefly due to a world-wide rise in commodity prices. As a result Britain and others now unhappily occupy the previously void 10–20 per cent inflation bracket referred to on p. 80. It remains to to be seen whether this is a permanent deterioration or if it is reversible as commodity prices level out or perhaps fall during the later part of 1974.

7

The International Payments Jungle

The balance of payments has been the bane of all post-war British governments, constraining their freedom of action, forcing them into distasteful and painful policies and thwarting the achievement of their principal economic objectives. If *only* the balance of payments could be got right ... But it never happens, except temporarily, and crisis follows crisis with heavy inevitability.

For ordinary people, it must often seem that Britain teeters on the verge of international bankruptcy. Strangely, it is the balance of payments statistics, so remote from everyday life, which have become the main index of our collective economic guilt, for politicians have not been slow to point out that it is our indolence, irresponsibility and antiquated attitudes and practices which are responsible for the country's international weakness. Month by month, the publication of the trade figures reminds us of our national shame.

To some degree, this obsessive preoccupation with the balance of payments is self-deception. There *are* real problems arising out of our international economic situation, though their nature and extent are commonly misunderstood. But before we can assess how important the balance of payments really is, we must firstly spell out the meaning of those figures which cause so much alarm and despondency.

'Balance of payments' is a term which is sometimes rather loosely used. It can refer to a variety of international accounts and it is important to be clear which of these is under discussion. The first of these accounts – and this is the one which the newscasters gravely announce month by month – is the *balance of visible trade*. What this consists of is all recorded transactions between residents of this country and non-residents which involve the exchange of merchandize. A glance at the British balance of trade does indeed suggest a persistent failure to pay our way. Take, for example, the decade 1959–69 (Table 3). In not *one* year did the United Kingdom manage to export sufficient to pay for its imports from abroad. Year after year, the balance of trade was in deficit, sometimes to the tune of over five hundred million pounds.

Table 3: United Kingdom Balance of Trade 1959–69 (£m.)

	1959	1960	1961	1962	1963	1964
Imports	3,639	4,138	4,043	4,095	4,362	5,003
Exports	3,522	3,732	3,891	3,993	4,282	4,486
Balance	−117	−406	−152	−102	−80	−517

	1965	1966	1967	1968	1969
Imports	5,042	5,211	5,576	6,807	7,153
Exports	4,817	5,168	5,122	6,273	7,056
Balance	−225	−43	−454	−534	−97

Despite the fact that the value of exports almost exactly doubled during these ten years, the outlay on imports always kept a step ahead, so that there was a persistent 'trade gap'. No one, of course, could expect imports to exactly *equal* exports every year, since they are the results of hundreds of thousands of independent decisions. But this was a decade of persistent deficit (although, for reasons which we shall discuss later, 1970 and 1971 were years of balance of trade surplus).

In fact, the trade gap is not, in itself, a matter of great concern. First of all, those who think it is a post-war phenomenom should consult the historical records; they will find that throughout the nineteenth century – at the height of the industrial revolution and when Britain had a head start in international trading – we regularly imported each year more merchandise than we exported. The same was true of the period up to 1945. What *is* novel about the post-war years is that the trade gap has, in proportionate terms, narrowed. Before the war, exports generally earned only about two-thirds of the foreign exchange needed to foot the import bill; recently, export earnings have been 90 per cent plus of the value of imports. (And years like 1956, 1970 and 1971, when there have been trade surpluses, are totally exceptional in the whole course of British economic history.) If the trade balance was the appropriate measure of international economic success, then Britain would seem to be doing very much better in recent years than it did in the past. But anyway, it *isn't* the proper yardstick – it is only one part of the total payments picture.

Another vital element is the trade in what are rather mysteriously called 'invisibles'. This refers to current transactions which involve payments between residents and non-residents but in which there is no exchange of physical goods. Firstly, such payments arise from the provision of services of one kind and another, such as shipping, civil aviation and tourism. If, for example, you spend your holiday in France travelling across the Channel on a French ferry, from the balance of payments viewpoint it is just as though you had imported goods from France into this country. A second important category of invisibles comprises interests, profits and dividend payments on past investments. Payments by Ford U.K. to its American shareholders represent an invisible import for the British economy (a payment from us to them); similarly, repatriated profits from subsidiaries of British firms abroad are invisible exports for us. Thirdly there are payments arising from the activities of the government. Outgoings under this heading (U.K. invisible imports) chiefly take the form of maintaining embassies and similar establishments in other countries, military expenditure abroad and official aid to underdeveloped countries. Against them must be set the payments to U.K. residents which arise from similar activities of foreign governments in this country.

Adding the net balance of such invisible items to the balance of visible trade yields what is known as the *balance of payments on current account*. Since net invisibles have always been favourable (we have always earned more under this heading than we have paid out), the U.K. international performance looks a little more respectable when judged by the current account than by visible trade alone. Fig. 22 looks again at the decade 1959–69 and shows that there were more years of surplus on current account than deficit, although the deficits were generally larger.

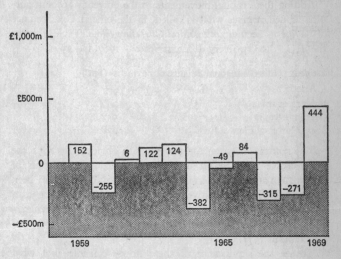

Figure 22. United Kingdom balance of payments on current account

The current account, like the balance of trade, is extremely unlikely actually to balance. Similarly, too, it cannot be used on its own to judge the economy's international success or failure. Still further sources of payments and receipts of foreign currency have to be added in before we can begin to evaluate the situation.

These take the form of *capital* movements. Americans, for example, may be (a) buying or building factories in Britain (direct investment); or (b) buying shares in British companies (portfolio investment); or (c) increasing their holdings of liquid assets in Britain (like bank balances) – to take advantage of higher interest rates, because they need them for trading purposes, or even because they expect the value of the pound to rise *vis-à-vis* the dollar. All of these represent an inflow of foreign currency. Against them must be set the outflow of foreign currency which arises from the corresponding efforts of British individuals, firms and government to increase their overseas assets.

Adding these capital movements to the currency account surplus or deficit gives what is called, in the official U.K. balance of payments accounts, the *Total Currency Flow*. Table 4 shows the T.C.F. for two very different years – 1967 and 1971.

Table 4: United Kingdom Balance of payments (£m.)

	1967	1971
Balance of trade	−552	297
Current account	−298	952
Total Currency Flow	−671	3,228

The contrast between the two years is obvious. By 1971 the 1967 visible trade deficit had been replaced by a surplus of £297m. An unfavourable current account of £298m. had been transformed into a positive balance of £952m. And the turn round in the Total Currency Flow was even more spectacular – from an outflow of £671m. in 1967 to a massive inflow of £3,228m. in 1971.

To see the significance of these flows, consider first what would happen in a world in which governments made no attempt to maintain any given external exchange rate for their currencies. Then the rate at which the pound would exchange against, for example, dollars would depend on the supply and demand of pounds coming onto the foreign exchange market where currencies are dealt in. Any sale of pounds (the supply coming from those who are buying dollars) would tend to depress the price of pounds in terms of dollars. Demand, on the other hand, people buying pounds with dollars, would push its price up. Fig 23 illustrates these pushes and pulls on the exchange rate.

The supply and demand of pounds on the foreign exchange market arise out of the various transactions which we have just been listing. U.K. residents will be coming to the market to buy dollars in order to pay Americans from whom they have bought visible or invisible imports; they will be *selling* pounds in ex-

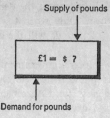

Supply of pounds

£1 = $?

Demand for pounds

Figure 23

change for dollars. Americans, on the other hand, will be buying pounds, with dollars, so that they can settle their accounts with U.K. residents who have exported to them. Capital flows will have a similar effect. American investment in the U.K. will mean increased demand for pounds, British investment overseas greater sales of pounds. Fig 24 shows how these various transactions fit into the picture.

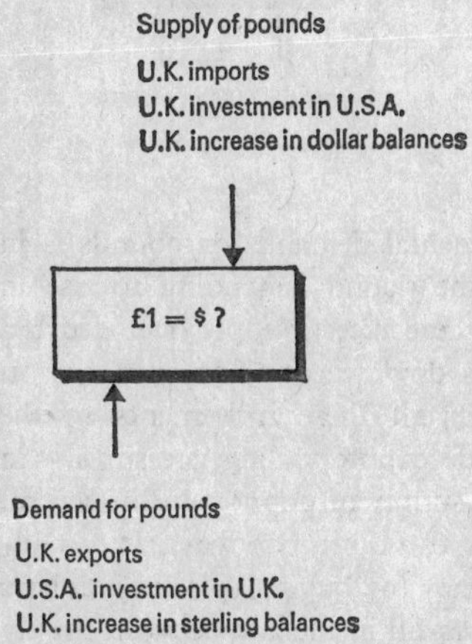

Supply of pounds

U.K. imports
U.K. investment in U.S.A.
U.K. increase in dollar balances

£1 = $?

Demand for pounds

U.K. exports
U.S.A. investment in U.K.
U.K. increase in sterling balances

Figure 24

If the supply of pounds exceeds the demand, the exchange rate will fall to bring the two into line – pounds will become cheaper in terms of dollars. Similarly, the rate at which pounds exchange for dollars will increase if the demand for pounds exceeds the supply of them. Only when the demand for pounds just equals the supply of pounds will the exchange rate remain constant.

However, in post-war years, governments have not generally allowed exchange rates to find their own level in this way. Under the International Monetary Fund Agreement, they have tried to maintain relatively fixed exchange rates between different currencies.

To see how they do this, imagine first a situation in which they were committed to *totally* fixed rates of exchange, for example £1 = $3. Fig. 25 shows two sets of circumstances:

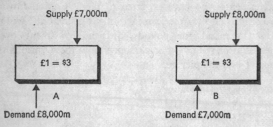

Figure 25

25A, in which the non-governmental demand for pounds is in excess of the supply, so that the pound is tending to rise in terms of the dollar; and 25B, where excess supply over demand is pushing the price of pounds downwards. The only way in which the government can prevent these movements in the exchange rate is to itself provide countervailing pressures – in the first case supplementing the supply of pounds, in the second augmenting the demand. This it can do in two ways. It can adjust its reserves of foreign currency (by buying or selling dollars in exchange for pounds); or it can fill in the gap between supply and demand by borrowing from or lending to other overseas monetary authorities like the U.S. government or the I.M.F.

Of course, in the case of a downward pressure on the exchange rate, the government's ability to maintain the original rate depends on its reserves of dollars with which it can counter any excess selling of pounds, and on the extent to which it can borrow from overseas monetary authorities. Both are likely to be limited.

We can now return to the 1967 and 1971 figures and see what they signify. In 1967, it will be remembered, the Total Currency Outflow was £671m. In 1971, there was a Total Currency Inflow of £3,228m.

A currency *outflow* means that at the existing exchange rate the supply of pounds exceeds the demand. In the absence of official intervention, the value of the pound would fall. What in fact happened in 1967 was that the government at first tried to match the outflow by 'official financing', in particular by allowing the reserves to fall and by massive borrowing from other governments. Subsequently, in November, it finally decided to devalue the pound, and allow the rate at which it would exchange for dollars to fall from 2.80 to 2.40.

In 1971, on the other hand, the massive currency inflow which took place would have represented an upward pressure on the value of the pound if the authorities had not intervened. What they did was to maintain the existing exchange rate and to use the inflow to build up official gold and foreign exchange reserves by over £1,500m. – and to make large repayments of debt to the International Monetary Fund and other monetary authorities.

So much for the technicalities – enough, it is hoped, to convince readers that international payments analysis is a complex matter and that simple references to a visible trade deficit as evidence of a balance of payments problem just won't do. But what *will* do? When is the balance of payments a problem?

The answer, in a nutshell, is this: the balance of payments is a problem when our total receipts of foreign exchange are too small or too unstable to allow us to do what we want to do. Look first at why the U.K. *needs* foreign exchange. Demand for it arises from a number of sources. (i) To buy imports of goods and services from abroad. Partly this is a matter of getting hold of goods which we don't produce ourselves in sufficient quantity – foodstuffs and raw materials. Partly it is simply that individuals and firms, for a variety of reasons, prefer foreign goods to those produced in this country. (ii) To finance overseas invest-ment. To the extent that it is thought a good thing that Britain should export capital overseas (building factories there or buying foreign securities) – with consequent benefit to the balance of payments in future years as profits, interest and dividends begin to flow back – the necessary foreign exchange has to be found. (iii) To finance a British diplomatic and military presence in various parts of the world. (iv) To enable the British govern-ment to maintain a flow of 'official aid' to underdeveloped countries. (v) To facilitate repayment of foreign debts accumu-lated in the past. (vi) To add to official reserves of gold and foreign exchange.

The sources of foreign exchange from which these needs can be met are also various: earnings from the export of goods and services, short-term and long-term capital inflows (private or official) and drawing on reserves. If the balance of payments is not to be seen as a problem, not only must these inflows of foreign exchange be of a sufficient *quantity* to meet require-ments. They must also be of an acceptable *quality*. Official policy might, for example, regard financing through increased short-term indebtedness as undesirable because of its inherent instability.

What is more, a satisfactory balance of payments has to be one which can be achieved without abandoning other economic objectives. Here, indeed, is the crux of the matter as British governments have seen it: how to keep the balance of payments right while simultaneously pursuing goals of full employment, expansion and reasonably stable prices. If balance of payments strength can be bought only at the price of higher domestic unemployment, it is a very dubious 'equilibrium'. Deflating the economy may certainly help the external situation, by depressing the demand for imports and perhaps inducing producers to seek export outlets more energetically in lieu of domestic sales. But this is only to conceal the underlying problem which be-comes exposed again as soon as the authorities try to reflate. At that stage, it is all too likely that imports will rise much more rapidly than exports, partly because increased supplies of raw materials are necessary *before* exports can be produced, partly because domestic production may not have expanded fast enough to meet increased consumption demands (as in the car industry during the consumer boom of 1972), and partly because the attractiveness of the home market weakens the export drive of British manufacturers. What governments have sought, therefore, is an external payments position strong enough to withstand these full-employment, expansionary pressures. What they have more generally managed is a balance of payments which can be maintained only at less than full capacity utilization.

What emerges from all these complexities is that a balance of payments 'problem' cannot be defined in any objective, technical, unequivocal way. It is all a matter of whether what is 'coming in' is sufficient (and of an acceptable form) to meet what it is the aim of economic policy to see 'going out' – and whether this can be achieved without forfeiting other policy goals. What constitutes 'balance of payments equilibrium' is a nationally subjective, highly political notion.

In these terms, it is certainly true that during the sixties Britain faced an increasingly severe balance of payments problem. It arose because earnings of foreign exchange on the current account fell further and further short of the amount necessary to pay for official external aims without recourse to unacceptable doses of deflation. But the problem arose not so much from a peculiarly British inability to export sufficiently as from the determination on the part of successive governments that the problem should be solved within a *given* political framework.

Thus it was felt right and proper that the U.K. should be a major overseas investor, maintain substantial defence postures in various parts of the world and offer considerable official aid to underdeveloped countries. All of these are clearly to a large degree *political* targets. Moreover, governments did all they could to achieve them within a context of fixed exchange rates. The external value of the pound was held as near-sacrosanct by Conservative and Labour governments alike. Primarily this attitude stemmed from a determination to maintain the role of sterling as an international currency – one not just used for domestic payments but one which foreigners, too, were prepared to hold as a means of settling their debts between themselves. It was argued that for sterling to be used in this way brought substantial economic benefits like the earnings of the City of London; but it was also seen as a source of political prestige – to put it bluntly, buying a seat at the conference table. However, given this use of sterling for international payments, the pound was in a highly exposed position. Recurrent balance of payments 'crises' could be all too easily manufactured. For as soon as foreigners, for whatever reason, thought that they could detect a weakness in the British position (or even a relative strength in other economies), they could switch funds out of the U.K. in a volume and at a speed which was quite alarming in relation to the British reserves which represented the major line of defence against such a speculative run on the pound.

If, then, there was a persistent balance of payments problem, it was a problem which to a large extent was of our own making. It was not international economics which somehow dictated that Britain should maintain extensive external commitments, encourage the use of sterling as an international currency and defend the pound at its existing rate. These were all policy aims on the part of successive governments – aims which other members of the international community were not always wholly sympathetic towards.

Within this framework of political aims, everything was tried. Time and again, growth of the domestic economy was repressed in order to alleviate pressure on the balance of payments. Structural policies to improve efficiency, incomes policy and deflation itself were designed to make all British industry more competitive with our international economic rivals.

What could not have been clear to the mass of British people was the extent to which the shortfall on the balance of payments was *marginal*. The biggest of the current account deficits was of the order of £500 million – which sounds a lot until it is related to imports of £8,000 million and a national income of £40,000 million. It seems extraordinary in retrospect that so many sacrifices were called for to rectify so minor a problem, and that it took so long before the framework of aims within which the balance of payments had to be solved was itself called into question. Could Britain *afford* to maintain so grandiose a role in world affairs? Just how important was it, after all, to defend a particular external value of the pound?

The breakthrough came, belatedly, with the 1967 devaluation. The object of devaluation is to make imports relatively more expensive (and therefore reduce their volume) and to make exports cheaper (in the hope that sufficiently more will be bought to yield higher foreign exchange earnings). It is allowed for in the rules of the I.M.F. whenever a country's balance of payments can be categorized as being in 'fundamental disequilibrium'. We have already noted the difficulties of defining equilibrium itself. Although certainly the British payments position could be seen as acutely inadequate to meet Britain's official aims and commitments, other countries could reasonably argue that it was time that Britain cut its international political ambitions according to its cloth. It was important therefore that in fact the 1967 devaluation was accompanied by such a reduction in external aims – the withdrawal from East of Suez and restrictions placed on the outward flow of British investment capital.

Judged by the 1967 and 1971 figures, devaluation could be heralded as a resounding success. However, it is difficult, firstly, to be sure how much of this improvement was the direct result of devaluation and how much it was due to other factors: a recent study by the National Institute suggests that about 60 per cent of the improvement in the current account was attributable to devaluation and that the price-responsiveness of both imports and exports was disappointingly below what had been expected.[1] And, secondly, it could be argued that the new-found strength of the balance of payments was partly artificial, as it was being achieved with the economy operating at well below full capacity.

Certainly, by 1972 a new crisis emerged. To some extent this could be attributed to the failure of the government to contain cost-inflationary pressures which whittled away a good deal of the competitive edge afforded by devaluation. Partly it was due to the attempt to maintain the readjustment pattern of exchange rates between industrialized countries laid down in the Smith-

1. 'The Effects of the Devaluation of 1967 on the Current Balance of Payments', N.I.E.S.R., *Economic Journal*, March 1972 (supplement).

sonian Agreement of November 1971. Whatever the cause, by June 1972 the British government faced a renewed speculative attack on the pound, which would lead to a flight from sterling and a decimation of the reserves unless help was forthcoming from other monetary authorities.

The government's response to this situation was an encouraging one. Instead of savagely deflating an economy already relatively depressed, instead of negotiating massive official support for the pound while watching reserves rapidly decline meanwhile, it simply allowed the pound to 'float' in the foreign exchange market and find its own level. This represented both a refusal to sacrifice domestic economic objectives to the exigencies of the international situation, and an acceptance of exchange-rate adjustments as a technical expedient rather than the hallmark of national humiliation which they had become during the sixties. Hopefully, here was the basis of an altogether more sensible approach to the balance of payments which could serve as a pattern for future years.

To some extent this is so. But optimism must be tempered on three counts. Firstly, a policy of greater exchange-rate flexibility – when, as in the British case, it is always a matter of downward movements – is not without its penalties. Each depreciation of the currency means that we have to export a greater volume of goods and services to acquire any given volume of imports. Moreover, in an economy as dependent on foreign trade as is the British, each increase in import prices serves as an additional cost-inflationary pressure, which in turn increases the likelihood that further adjustments to the exchange rate will be needed in the future. It is this relationship between the balance of payments and inflation which makes it urgently necessary to seek new approaches to the problem of keeping incomes and prices under control.

Secondly, the British balance of payments 'problem' has to be solved within an international monetary framework which remains alarmingly primitive in comparison with the highly sophisticated *domestic* monetary systems which have evolved in mature economics. As we have seen, what each country regards as 'equilibrium' in its balance of payments stems to a large extent from its political aims and ambitions. Unfortunately, there is no way of guaranteeing that the target current-account surpluses of one group of countries is precisely or even roughly matched by the target current-account deficits of others. Given the probable incompatibility between the two sets of plans, remedial action by one country to 'right' its position is all too likely to lead to retaliatory adjustments elsewhere in the system. The fact that we can't all simultaneously achieve what we want is a perfect recipe for continued international payments disturbances and uncertainty. Sooner or later, fundamental international monetary reform will have to take place if order is to be brought to the international jungle.

Thirdly, there are the implications of Britain joining Europe. On the long-term agenda is the creation of a single European monetary system, which in some ways offers scope for coping with some of the problems which we have just been discussing. But there is a disturbing aspect to the prospect of full monetary union, which is that member countries will ultimately have to forfeit the right to alter exchange rates between themselves. Balance of payments problems will not thereby be eliminated. Instead they will become internal rather than external matters. The fact that Scotland, for example, is part of the British monetary system does not mean that Scotland cannot get into balance of payments difficulty. Indeed it does just that – there is a chronic tendency for Scottish imports from the rest of the country to exceed Scottish exports. If no official action was taken, balance would only be brought about by a reduction in the level of Scottish incomes, and a relative impoverishment of that part of the country. It is the purpose of British regional policy to counterbalance these tendencies – to create a system of inducements which artificially simulate the effects of devaluing the Scottish currency against the rest of the economy.

Similarly, Britain, as part of a European monetary union, would no longer be able to adjust its balance of payments through exchange-rate changes. The brunt of any necessary adjustment would have to fall on the domestic economy. If Britain has a tendency to inflate more rapidly than its European partners, or if productivity here rises less rapidly, the prospect of Britain consequently becoming the 'poor man of Europe' is a real one. Given the difficulties which we have had in achieving regional balance *within* the U.K. it is hard to be optimistic that a European regional policy can be devised which is sufficiently vigorous to counter this tendency. Ironically, then, at the very moment when governments have at long last acquired a new boldness in exchange-rate policy, the U.K. has undertaken a European commitment which may ultimately imprison it still further and make the balance of payments an economic problem rather than a largely political one.

Postscript (1974). During 1973–4 the U.K. balance of payments rapidly worsened. From a small surplus in 1972 the current account moved into a £1,470 million deficit in 1973 – with estimates of a further deterioration of up to £4,000 million in 1974. This was due to the downward float of sterling coupled with the dramatic rise which took place in world commodity prices, particularly petroleum. Hopefully the problem will prove to be only short-term, with (a) the volume of British exports increasing substantially as a result of their price-competitive advantage created by sterling depreciation, and (b) the 'oil deficit' financed by short-term borrowing in the period up to 1980 when it is expected that Britain will be able to meet the whole of its petroleum requirements from the North Sea.

8

Getting Richer

By 1956, a British government confidently committed itself in a White Paper to securing 'a rapid and sustained rate of economic growth'. Governments ever since have been desperately trying to fulfil that commitment. However, to think that rapid growth was even possible was a far cry from the pessimism of the pre-war stagnationist pundits who argued that mature economies such as Britain had finally run out of steam and that there was little further scope for squeezing greater output from our limited resources.

That is not to say that there is anything new about the post-war interest in economic growth. On the contrary, it was just this problem – the dynamics of *developing* an economy – which was of prime concern to the founding fathers of modern economics in the eighteenth and early nineteenth centuries. It was this very matter – the 'causes of the wealth of nations' and how that wealth could be increased – which largely occupied Adam Smith and his immediate successors. Only in the latter part of the last century were economists diverted from this central aim into an examination of the minutiae of the economic system, the detailed rules for an optimum allocation of resources within a *given* boundary of production possibilities. And, of course, with the unemployment of the 1920s and 1930s, questions of expanding the economy's capacity to produce seemed quite irrelevant when even its current capacity couldn't be fully used.

These days we have come to expect that year by year the economy will grow richer. What we are concerned about is why it doesn't do so faster. These expectations have been nurtured by politicians with competing promises that it is *they* who have the key to improved economic performance. And despite continuous disappointments at the limited accomplishments of successive governments, the economic horizons of the mass of people remain optimistic. Most of us would be surprised if our children did not live in an even more affluent society than our own.

Chapter 10 casts some preliminary doubts on the extent to which economic growth can properly be regarded as an end of policy. In this chapter we are largely concerned with the nature and causes of growth. To begin with, we should define what it is that we are talking about.

Thus, for example, if the total value of goods and services produced in Britain this year is £50,000m. and in a year's time it has risen to £55,000m., it appears that the capacity of the economy to produce output has gone up by 10 per cent. However, part of that rise may merely reflect inflation. If the prices of the goods and services which go to make up the gross national product have risen on average by, say 7 per cent the *real* increase in output (as opposed to its money value) is only 3 per cent. This is the growth rate for the economy – although, apart from eliminating the effects of changes in the general price level, we might also want to allow for population increase. If, for example, population has grown by 1 per cent over the course of the year, the growth rate per capita is reduced to only 2 per cent.

Confusion sometimes arises because there are two broad sources of increased output which are not always clearly distinguished. Firstly, production can be increased when the economy starts off with unemployment and idle capacity; this was the problem that Keynes was largely concerned with – how to ensure that an economy works at its full potential. And, secondly, increased output can be brought about if the potential itself is increased through greater efficiency in squeezing more goods and services out of our limited resources. It is the second of these, the 'growth of productive potential', which mostly interests us here. Measuring it involves comparing like with like, output in years when the margin of unused capacity in the economy is the same – say, 3 per cent. If, in another year, that margin is reduced to 2 per cent, clearly there will be an additional increment of output. But that will be in the nature of a once-and-for-all bonus – quite different from the effect of increasing the productive potential. In practice, politicians in particular are very happy to mix the two sources of increased output together in order to yield the highest possible overall growth rate for the economy.

Three further general points should be made at this stage. Firstly, growth measures the increase in output of all goods and services – it says nothing about *which* sorts of production have expanded, at what costs or who gets the benefit; it is a highly aggregative concept. Secondly, given the difficulties of measuring all that goes to make up a national output of some £50,000 million (and of deflating the total to allow for general price changes), it is not surprising that ostensibly precise statistical statements (for instance that the economy in the past year grew at 2·7 per cent) are in fact subject to a significant margin of error. Sometimes it is doubtful whether, for example, the economy grew very slightly or marginally slipped back. Finally, an initial warning that, although economic growth is commonly equated by politicians and others with 'economic progress' or an 'increase in the economic welfare of the community' or an 'improvement in the standard of living', it does not in fact necessarily indicate any of these.

How we should interpret growth figures and how far economic growth should be a prime economic objective are matters which will be returned to later. For the rest of this chapter we shall concentrate simply on facts and theories about growth.

First of all, how well or badly has the British economy been performing in this respect? Certainly, there is a general feeling that failure to get the economy on a path of sustained expansion has been one of the many signs of a chronic British economic malaise. But is this view really justified? It depends on what is used as a yardstick for assessing the recent record.

To see Britain's post-war growth performance in the most favourable light, we should look backwards. Table 5 shows that

Table 5: G.D.P. per capita. Annual % increase

1870–1913	1·6
1922–38	1·1
1950–57	1·7
1957–65	2·4
1963–70	2·7

judged by what we achieved in the past, recent growth rates per capita looked decidedly commendable.

A growth rate of 2·7 per cent – the annual average for 1963–70 – is a great improvement on what was managed at any other time during the previous century, including the industrial revolution, when Britain had a head start on other nations. And it should also be remembered that growth takes place at a *compound* rate: 2·7 per cent a year is enough to double the national output every quarter of a century.

Pessimists, on the other hand, should seek their comparisons elsewhere. That similar economies have fared very much better than the U.K. is shown in Table 6. Even if we set aside the quite spectacular record of Japan, it is clear that countries much closer to home have all managed to achieve substantially higher rates of economic growth than we have. Depressingly, Britain is found to be propping up the international league table.

Table 6: Rates of growth, 1955–68

Country	G.D.P.	G.D.P. per capita employed
Japan	9·7	8·3
France	5·5	4·9
Italy	5·3	5·8
Germany	5·0	4·3
Sweden	4·5	3·4
Canada	4·4	1·9
Belgium	3·9	3·5
USA	3·9	2·4
UK	2·8	2·3

Source: O.E.C.D., *The Growth of Output 1960–80* (1970).

Why the British economy has grown slowly is a question to which a very large number of economists (and not just British) have devoted a good deal of their attention. As a result, there is no shortage of answers. Indeed there is an embarrassing number of them – the host of factors which have been put forward as relevant must grossly *over*-explain the problem. But, despite this wealth of analysis, the truthful answer to the question is that we simply don't know.

At an elementary level, it is possible to construct a model of the economy in which investment and savings are the key to faster growth. On this argument, growth depends on the rate at which capital can be accumulated. Suppose to begin with that the economy is producing an output of £50,000 million a year with a capital stock (of factories, machines, roads, mines, etc.) of £150,000 million. In other words, for every three units of capital it has, it produces one unit of output (in economic jargon, the capital-output ratio is 3 : 1). If it is hoped that in the coming year output can be expanded by £2,500m. (i.e. a growth rate of 5 per cent on the initial G.N.P. of £50,000m.), then capital stock will have to be increased by three times that amount – new investment will have to be undertaken of the order of £7,500 million. But where does this new investment come from? It requires resources which, in a fully employed economy, must be released from their alternative use in present consumption. The implication of getting the economy onto a higher long-term growth trend is that we shall have to make some short-term sacrifices. A larger national cake in the future means limiting our consumption of it today. Higher savings channelled into productive investment is the path to faster growth. The British economy has grown slowly because we have not been prepared to limit our demands on resources *now* in order to have more jam tomorrow.

Economists and economic commentators who hold this view will point to the fact that investment in the British economy has been significantly lower than in West European countries. But comparisons of this kind are extremely difficult to make. Enormous problems arise in measuring everything that goes to make up the capital stock of a country. Should we concentrate on the figures for simply *net* investment (the addition to the total stock) or *gross* investment (new investment plus that needed to maintain the previous stock)? Numerous complications arise, particularly in the treatment of depreciation.

Putting to one side these purely technical problems, the fact is that anyway no very close correlation can be established between investment rates and economic growth in various countries. And, even if they could, the appropriate causal relationship would still have to be established. Would it be investment which was *caus-*

ing growth, or the growth of output which itself led to higher investment?

The answer is not known. What is obvious is that investment is very much a hold-all concept. Whether additions to the capital stock result in faster growth must depend on what sort of investment is being undertaken. The impact on output of building new hospitals, new office blocks or new factories is not likely to be the same. Again, the extent to which new capital is used effectively may be as important a consideration as the total itself. The age structure of the capital stock is also important; part of the post-war success of the continental countries may be attributable to the fact that they were unfortunate enough to suffer much greater wartime destruction of their capital assets than we did and consequently were forced to replace them by more efficient and up-to-date equipment.

What has become clear from the researches of those interested in the question of why growth rates between economies differ is that there are multiple influences to take into account. There is no single economic variable which can be manipulated to break through from a low to a faster rate of economic growth. Professor E. F. Denison, for example, in his mammoth study of *Why Growth Rates Differ*,[1] suggests no less than sixteen different relevant factors and tries to measure their relative significance. Of these we will look briefly at just three.

Firstly, perhaps Britain is no longer big enough to keep up in the growth race. Efficiency and productivity, it is argued, depend essentially on the size of firm, and that, in turn, depends on the size of market for which it is catering. 'The division of labour,' as Adam Smith put it a long time ago, 'is limited by the size of market.' Only with markets as large as those in the United States or the Soviet bloc can full advantage be taken of modern technology.

Certainly it is true that dramatic reductions in unit costs of production can often be achieved by mass production. What is doubtful, however, is whether there are many lines of production in which the U.K. domestic market of 55 million plus its export potential are inadequate to support a fully efficient form of pro-

1. Brookings Institution, Washington, 1967.

duction. Aircraft, computers, atomic-energy plants are some of the more obvious areas in which conceivably this is so. But those who advocated British entry into Europe principally on the grounds that a market of 300 million would at last ensure that Britain would be fully able to exploit the 'economies of large-scale production' have little in the way of hard evidence on which to rest their case. On the contrary, British firms are already, at least in comparison with European competitors, large-scale. Economies of scale can only be exploited when the market is *standardized* as well as simply large – and it is by no means clear that this will be so given varied European tastes. And size in itself is no guarantee of greater efficiency: much depends on the motivations which have induced greater industrial concentration.

Another and rather more plausible explanation of the discrepancy between British growth rates and those of continental European countries emphasizes the structural differences between economies. The fact that E.E.C. countries have managed much more substantial growth than the U.K. may be attributable to their relative 'economic immaturity'. While in Britain the proportion of the working population engaged in agriculture, for example, was about 3 per cent, the position in the Six was very different, as can be seen from Fig. 3. The figure also shows how the share of agricultural in total employment drastically fell between 1958 and 1968.

Table 7: Percentage Shares of Agricultural Employment in Total Employment

	1958	1968
Belgium	8·1	5·8
France	23·7	15·8
Germany	15·7	10·2
Italy	34·9	22·5
Netherlands	12·6	7·9
E.E.C.	22·6	14·5

Source: N.I.E.S.R.

This shift in occupational distribution may well have been

a significant element in the growth process. Agriculture is a sector in which productivity has historically been much lower than in manufacturing industry. It is inherently less susceptible to the application of modern scientific technology and the economies of large-scale production. Therefore, countries which began the post-war period with a relatively high proportion of their working population in agriculture had a reservoir of low-productivity labour which could be drawn into higher-productivity occupations as the industrial sector expanded. This was a growth source which was not available to economies like Britain, in which surplus agricultural labour had already been largely absorbed by manufacturing industry. On this argument, recent differences in growth rates between Britain and Europe are accountable in terms of a once-and-for-all increase in productivity which the European countries experienced by being initially rather 'backward'.

A third candidate for the part of villain of the piece is the possibility that the British authorities may have been peculiarly bad at managing the economy. We have already seen that demand management during the post-war period has been largely directed towards the achievement of stability – eradicating the cycle, maintaining full employment and trying to keep price rises within reasonable proportions while at the same time achieving balance of payments equilibrium. This has been no easy task. Have, therefore, failures in demand management themselves been at least partly responsible for the relatively weak British growth record? Or is there a basic conflict between the various policy objectives?

Two points need to be made. Firstly, it is evident that during the post-war period Britain has not even managed to achieve a growth rate consistent with its underlying trend of productivity. Given stop–go in terms of economic management, many years have witnessed an economy operating well below its true potential. Every 1 per cent shortfall from the underlying growth potential would have paid for a Concorde development project, or, more sensibly, for 200,000 low-cost housing units. Although the clumsiness of demand-management techniques are partly responsible, below-possible growth rates have resulted chiefly from real or imagined conflicts between the various policy objectives. Successive governments felt that to run the economy at a level of demand which would ensure full exploitation of the growth potential might lead to either (a) an acceleration in the rate of inflation or (b) balance of payments difficulties as imports were sucked in at a faster rate than exports were stimulated. However, what has been said in earlier chapters casts doubts on the validity of the deflationary policy conclusions which were drawn from this analysis. Trying to control demand inflation by deflationary measures can, as we have seen, merely add fuel to a cost-inflationary fire. And we have further argued that the apparent conflict between growth and balance of payments equilibrium was principally due to over-ambitious foreign commitment together with an obsessive determination to defend the external value of the pound. The losses in potential output can be regarded with some justification therefore as the price of policy mistakes rather than the result of an inevitable conflict between basic economic objectives.

Moreover, the erratic course of economic activity in Britain over the years may well have been an independent source of the slow rate of growth. Stop–go is not very conducive in getting people to adopt attitudes and to take decisions likely to increase the growth rate. A general expectation that in the near future there will be a cutback in the level of activity in the economy is not one which encourages forward-looking policies on the part of either business management or trade unions. Uncertainty breeds doubt and suspicion – and a determination to hold on to what already they have rather than a willingness to seek future improvements. Confidence may be an important element in determining the rate of growth of an economy. Assured that sustained growth *will* take place, firms are much more likely to be interested in preparing and implementing long-term investment programmes, in introducing new products and processes; workers, in a full-employment situation of steady growth, may be much more receptive to the idea of changing practices and techniques. Reduction in the uncertainties of the future was one of the aims of the British experiments with 'indicative' planning in the 1960s – the sort of planning which, rather than coercing the various elements in the economy, hoped to bring about changes through mutual consent.

It was argued that if only the *feasibility* of faster growth could be demonstrated – if the various parties could only be shown the *compatibility* of their interests – then we could ultimately *talk* ourselves into a higher growth trend. But the plans failed, partly because the participants in the plans remained unconvinced and preferred to wait and see what the outcome would be, and partly because they were right to remain unconvinced since governments continued to adopt policies which in themselves doomed the plans to failure.

In the end, as someone has written, analyses of the causes of economic growth are inevitably reduced to exercises in 'amateur sociology'. Professor Denison's study, already referred to, concluded that the difference of growth rates between various countries could be only partially explained in terms of quantifiable economic factors. There remained a substantial 'residual element' which still had to be accounted for. It is not difficult to think of factors which might comprise this residual.

Some would lay the blame on the backwardness of British management: its failure to employ sufficient technical expertise and to use modern management techniques. Others see the root of the trouble in restrictive labour practices inherited from the very different conditions of the pre-war period. Others, again, would single out the amateurism of the governmental machine – at both parliamentary and civil-service levels – as a major anti-growth element. There is no shortage of anecdotal evidence to support these alternative views.

But similar material could easily be collected in other economies which have nonetheless managed higher growth rates than we have. Is there any reason why socio-economic factors should play a greater part in Britain than elsewhere?

Perhaps there is. The Brookings Institution report on the outlook for the British economy,[2] emphasized the extent to which Britain remains sharply stratified by class. As outside observers, this group of American economists stressed the dilettantism of British industry and the deep-rooted bifurcation of the educa-

2. R. E. Caves (ed.), *Britain's Economic Prospects*, Allen & Unwin, 1968.

tional and social system into 'them' and 'us'. If they are right, the result is that British businessmen simply do not take business sufficiently seriously to be as efficient as their counterparts elsewhere; that British labour, in squabbling about the share-out of the present national cake, retards its further growth; that both are regulated by authorities who lack any real understanding of either. We fail to grow faster because of the make-up of our social system rather than because of any simple economic deficiency.

When interest first arose in the problems of underdeveloped countries, it was felt that the lessons of growth in rich countries could be readily applied to solve the problems of the poor nations. To begin with, it was felt that the answer to their poverty lay simply in the injection of sufficient quantities of capital. Fashions changed and a new emphasis was placed on the importance of education – the growth of 'human capital'. Only in recent years have we come to realize that the process of transforming a traditional society requires a fundamental adjustment to the human attitudes, the structures and institutions which it embodies. The choice may be a painful one. If poor countries want real development, a major upheaval in traditional customs and practices is often the price which has to be paid.

It is perhaps time that the lesson was applied in reverse. Decade by decade, without any major change in government policies or the structure of the economy, the British economy is likely to continue to grow. There are forces making for growth already built into the economic system. But if we are dissatisfied with the present 'natural' rate of growth, then really it is *development* which we are seeking – shifting the economy from one level of growth to another and higher trend. It is doubtful whether that can be achieved merely by the manipulation of economic variables. Almost certainly what will be required are major changes in the underlying social system. These may be changes which result in us becoming more 'dynamic', more ruthless in our approach to business, more professional, more mobile. Given such a choice as that, perhaps faster growth is not worth it after all. Or is it possible that changes could be brought about in a more, rather than a less, humane environment?

We shall return to these matters later. For the time being we must look more closely at what we are trying to achieve. So far, we have assumed uncritically that full employment, faster growth, price and balance of payments stability *are* the proper objectives of economic policy. It is time to cast some preliminary doubts on whether this is so.

9

Beyond Full Employment

Of all the post-war objectives of economic policy, maintaining a high level of employment has been held the most sacrosanct. In recent years there has been much discussion about just how compatible full employment is with other objectives such as halting inflation, getting the balance of payments right and achieving rapid economic growth. Governments have at times flirted with the idea that there may be awkward 'trade-offs' between the various desiderata – that, for example, curbing price increases may involve having a somewhat larger pool of unemployed. Mistaken though they may have been, governments have not always even aimed at maximizing employment. But the level of 'politically acceptable' unemployment, although it may have risen, remains extremely low in comparison with what was customary in the pre-war period.

This is as it should be. Unemployment, quite apart from being absurdly wasteful, has been the most humanly degrading feature of twentieth-century capitalism. It is an evil which the increased economic understanding of the Keynesian revolution has made it possible for governments largely to eradicate. The record is not as good as it might have been. As we have already seen, Keynesian techniques have severe limitations when it comes to the fine tuning of the economy and dealing with the more structural problem of regional unemployment. Nonetheless, the employment performance of the economy over the past twenty-five years is dramatically better than it has ever been before.

However, with that said, how far does it make sense to continue to regard full employment as an end of economic policy? *Why* do people demand the right to work? For the majority, their jobs are simply the unavoidable drudge by which they earn incomes to maintain an acceptable level of consumption, to enjoy their leisure, to save for the future. Only for a lucky few is their work a source of personal satisfaction or fulfilment. In either case, employment is surely primarily a *means* rather than an end; we work in order to achieve a variety of ends. It is time that we evolved from thinking of full employment as a prime policy objective to greater concern with the *nature* of employment.

For Keynes, wrestling with the illogicality of an economic system gone so radically wrong as to throw millions out of work, employment creation was a necessary condition for saving the capitalist system itself. Given the fact that the greater part of unemployment was due solely to demand deficiency, *any* increased activity would be sufficient to generate a multiplied effect on employment levels. Pay men to dig holes in the ground and fill them up again, and their increased spending would stimulate increased output and employment in more productive occupations. As Keynes pointed out, earlier economic systems had stumbled upon their solutions to the problem: 'Ancient Egypt was doubly fortunate, and doubtless owed to this its fabled wealth, in that it possessed *two* activities, namely, pyramid building as well as the search for precious metals, the fruits of which, since they could not serve the needs of man by being consumed, did not stale with abundance. The Middle Ages built cathedrals and sang dirges.' Today, the arms race and lunar exploration are the modern equivalents. If it is simply a matter of creating jobs, a way can always be found of doing so. But, as Keynes went on to point out: 'It is not reasonable, however, that a sensible community should be content to remain dependent on such fortuitous and often wasteful mitigations when once we understand the influences upon which effective demand depends.'[1]

Concentrating on the overall employment total conceals the question of what employment is *for* – what it is that people are producing when they work. This is a matter which we shall be looking at in the following chapter. It is also important to

1. J. M. Keynes, *General Theory of Employment, Interest and Money*, p. 131.

ask questions about the *content* of work. What is happening to its intensity and tempo? How far does the work which people do afford them interest and satisfaction? Do their jobs leave them with the capacity fully to enjoy their leisure? How easy is it for people to find, not just any jobs, but jobs which they think match their abilities and temperaments? Looking into these aspects of employment which lie behind the mere counting of heads, the performance of modern industrial economies is a good deal less satisfactory than its record of relatively 'full employment' suggests.

High Technology and Employment

This is an age of exploding technologies. Industry today is more closely related to science than ever before, and the result is an ever more rapidly flowing stream of new products and new production processes. What are the effects of such rapid technical progress on employment?

Taking a broad view, the benefits from technical change have clearly been enormous. First of all, it has been possible through mechanization to replace a whole host of dirty, unpleasant, physically demanding jobs which were once done by men and women. Moreover, the increase in material well-being over the past centuries must be attributed, above all, to increased division of labour. Specialization by workers in particular tasks has been the major cause of the enormous increases in productivity which have taken place. Apart from the obvious improvements in efficiency which come from specialization through greater dexterity and learning through experience greater division of labour means job *simplification*. And once that happens, once a complex production process is broken down into its component parts, it is possible to introduce mechanization.

But what has been lost in the process? It is easy nostalgically to extoll the virtues of an idyllic pre-industrial age.

Two centuries ago, before the 'industrial revolution' was properly launched, a skilled workman in this country was a craftsman. Whether he worked in wood, clay, leather, stone, metal or glass, he was the master of his material, and the thing he produced grew in his hands from the substance of the earth to the finished article. He was ever-mindful that he was a member of an honoured craft; that he had reached his position after a long apprenticeship; and he took legitimate pride in the excellence of his work . . . Whatever else may have been lacking in that smaller scale of society in which the yeoman tilled the soil and masters and apprentices worked with patient skill at this craft, there was always this unassailable self-respect and, therefore, that abiding sense of security which is no common thing in the feverish jostling world of today'.[2]

Well, perhaps it wasn't *quite* like that. But there is nonetheless enough substance in the point for us to ask whether the division of labour in modern industrial societies has now proceeded to a degree which is almost self-defeating. Where work has been reduced to the endless repetition of a simple mindless task, where workers are little more than machine-minders, is it any longer possible to take pride in one's work or to derive any creative satisfaction from it?

The matter can be viewed first of all from the aspect of sheer economic efficiency. Workers utterly remote from the final product, engaged in what they consider an inevitable but meaningless drudge, are not likely to approach their work particularly conscientiously or responsibly. Mistakes are made, but nobody very much cares. (It is said about cars, for example, that the real 'duds' are those which come off the Monday assembly line.) The upshot is that either more resources have to be devoted to elaborate inspection procedures to maintain quality control, or the quality of the final product is unreliable. Moreover, the pent-up frustrations of endlessly monotonous working patterns must in the end boil over. Disputes, stoppages and industrial tension are at least partly attributable to the need to break the monotony of an otherwise never-ending routine.

These are facts which are now beginning to be recognized by industrial managements. In the nineteenth century it took a long time before employers realized that higher wages, far from pricing them into bankruptcy, were in fact a source of higher profits from greater productivity. Workers who earned enough to feed

2. E. J. Mishan, *The Costs of Economic Growth*, Penguin Books, 1969, pp. 206–9.

and look after themselves adequately turned out, incredibly, to be better at doing their jobs. Similarly today, there are enterprises where it is appreciated that greater job satisfaction may be an important element in further productivity increase.

The Volvo company in Sweden, for example, is currently building a car plant at Kalmar which will challenge all the traditional principles which have dominated motor-car economics since Henry Ford. What they are doing is no less than to abandon the conventional assembly line, manned by workers each performing repetitively a simple task as the car passes by and having little or no contact with those working alongside them. Instead, Volvo see the work-force as split into groups of between fifteen and twenty-five. The assembly line will be replaced by a system of components shunted round on electric trollies which will be moved into the groups' working bays when required. The work which the group performs will be a major production stage – the installation, for instance, of a complete electrical system. How they do it, how they divide the work amongst themselves, is up to them.

This is anti-specialization. In terms of capital outlay, the Kalmar factory will cost nearly 10 per cent more than the traditional lay-out. But Volvo are clearly hoping that the new experiment will contribute towards reducing some of the problems which have plagued them and other motor-car manufacturers in the past – widespread absenteeism and high labour turnover (the particularly traumatic year for Volvo was 1969, with an incredible 52 per cent turnover in its work-force). On top of that, Volvo have had increasing difficulty in attracting people to work in the factories at all. With higher education and living standards than our own, Swedish workers have spurned the monotony of the assembly line, and Swedish industry is increasingly manned by Finns and Yugoslavs.

In other words, Volvo are hoping that the new approach will *pay*. Such experiments – and there are a sprinkling of others – are wholly to be welcomed. But that does not mean that we should neglect situations in which job enrichment may *not* pay. Surely as a society we are now rich enough for methods of humanizing work to be thought worthwhile in themselves.

What we have to do is to get away from thinking that big is necessarily good, that massive scale and extreme specialization are technological imperatives. There *is* an alternative technology which would evolve once workers (and managers) were regarded as individuals rather than faceless 'labour inputs'. But efforts in this direction in devising more humanized techniques are bound to be limited until the nature of work is emphasized as the proper objective of employment policy.

Take, for example, the question of the hours which people work. Present techniques generally demand great regularity – so many hours per day (or, in some cases, per night), so many days a week and so many weeks a year. But why? Why shouldn't individuals be allowed to work the *number* of hours they like, and *when* they like? Here again, a start has already been made by a number of firms on the continent and in this country (for example Pilkingtons and I.C.I.) in piloting schemes which give employees a certain amount of choice about their daily starting and finishing times and their total working time per month.[3] So far they have been confined to administrative staff – those parts of the firms which are largely labour-intensive. Certainly it would be much more difficult to extend the principle to manufacturing production, where workers combine with highly expensive capital equipment. But once the principle was accepted, technology would have to be adapted accordingly. And this is as it should be – that technology adjusts to people rather than the other way round.

The nature of the work people do is closely related to the importance which they attach to leisure and the ways in which they use it. It was Marx who said that 'the production of too many useful things results in too many useless people'. The ethos of the modern industrial economy creates the danger that in their striving to acquire more and more goods people will become increasingly incapable of enjoying them. With their sensitivity blunted by the dull boredom of their working environment, it is not surprising that many have such difficulty in adjusting to retirement or using their time off in a satisfying

3. *Flexible Working Hours*, Information Report No. 12, Institute of Personnel Management, 1972.

way. Once again, as Galbraith points out, greater flexibility of working hours has an important contribution to make towards creating a more positive attitude towards leisure opportunities:

The employed person should be accorded a much wider set of options than at present between work and goods on the one hand and leisure on the other. But the options should not be confined to the work week. This is a poor unit around which to organize the effective use of leisure time; it has long been a perquisite of high social, educational or financial position that life – holidays, travel, tasks – is planned in terms of months or years. All individuals, in return for a lower annual pay, should have the option of several months' paid vacation. And all should similarly have the option of extended leaves of absence. The employees exercising these options would not be favoured in compensation per hour worked. What they are offered is the opportunity of choosing absence and exemption from toil in various forms as an alternative to earnings. There would be some inconvenience. But to fail to allow such choice – to be guided by the belief that everyone should work a standard week and year – is to make the needs of the industrial system, not the opportunity of the individual to fashion his own existence, the ruling social concern. Men who speak much of liberty should allow and even encourage it.[4]

In particular what this vista opens up is the possibility of a new approach to education. At present education is largely confined to the years preceding working life. But there is no reason why it should not be an ongoing process to which people can return as and when they please. Here, too, it is Sweden which has pioneered the notion that equality of opportunity means equal chances for young and old alike. Their 'second-path' philosophy ensures that there is a wide range of educational openings for adults, either to return to secondary schools or for mature entry into the universities or for industrial retraining.

A final aspect of enhancing the nature of employment is that of participation. We have already discussed the need for a technology which makes workers less remote from the final product. But that in itself is not enough. For them to be *involved* in the productive process, they must also feel that they have some say both in the objectives of the enterprise and the ways in which

4. J. K. Galbraith, *The New Industrial State*, Penguin Books, 1969, p. 369.

E.R.W.–7

it achieves them. This is a matter to which we shall return in Chapter 18.

Machines or Men?

Looked at from a management point of view, enriching the nature of work may seem an unnecessarily inconvenient, expensive, or even impractical matter. A more obvious way of dealing with the problem of alienated workers is simply to employ as few as possible of such unreliable inputs. Increasingly, technological change has made it possible for capital to be substituted for labour. In recent decades, the process has been given a new dimension with the development of automated production. Automation is distinguished from mechanization in that computerization enables machines to take over areas of decision-taking and rectifying errors as well as the more mundane operations. What will be the effects of automation on employment and its nature?

On the whole economists are inclined to take an optimistic view of the probable outcome. They regurgitate the arguments which they put forward against the nineteenth-century Luddites. Then, it was claimed, mechanization was bound to cause unemployment. No, said the economists. What will happen is that mechanization will lead to higher productivity and falling prices. At lower prices, more goods will be bought – and both more machines *and* more workers will be required. In the end, the economists were right, although there was a great deal of temporary technological unemployment and social distress during the transitional period to industrialization.

But is the argument equally applicable to the sort of technological revolution through which we are now passing? There are a number of reasons for doubting that this is so.

(i) The labour saving involved in automated production is of a quite different *order* from what has gone before. This is true both quantitatively (the reduction in work-force needed can be quite dramatic) and qualitatively – because automation does not make just unskilled and semi-skilled workers redundant but extends into the echelons of lower management itself.

The economists' principle might still hold good. Reduced

prices might stimulate demand to a level at which it would still be possible for everyone to be employed in automated plants. But the level of production which that would entail would have to be of quite astronomical proportions. Perhaps demand *could* be created to absorb that output. But would it make sense to do so? Is there *no* limit to our material acquisitiveness or to the natural resources which would be needed?

(ii) Enormous quantities of capital would be required to generate full employment at the new high-level technology. But there is no guarantee that this build-up of capital could be achieved at the same rate as labour is disgorged from traditional forms of production. Time-lags might be very considerable, and indeed there is evidence that already investment in modern technology is proving inadequate to provide sufficient new jobs.

(iii) Current unemployment as we have seen is largely concentrated in the unskilled, young and aged groups of workers who, in a modern technological economy, have depressingly little to offer. Automation will make redundant more of these workers, those with what are now regarded as considerable mechanical skills, and also clerical and lower management staff. If they are to be re-employed, they will have to learn new and appropriate skills. But, as Mishan puts it, 'it is far from being impossible that in the not-too-distant future a large proportion of the adult population would be *unemployable* simply because they would not be endowed with the innate capacities necessary to acquire the highly developed mental skills which may be called for by a more complex technology.' [5]

(iv) An obvious way of avoiding the dangers of technological unemployment on a large scale is for us to take the benefits of higher productivity not just in increased output but also in greater leisure. The way round the problem, in other words, is for *work-sharing*. The three-day week, the four-hour day – these are the prospects which are opened up by automated production. However, it is not a very likely outcome in a market economy with powerful and sectional trade unions. It is much more probable that trade unions in modern technological industries (representing as they do the interests of their current members

5. Mishan, op. cit., p. 228.

rather than potential members or the working class as a whole)
will work to limit the spread of employment, by achieving high
wages for their own workers. They are, after all, in a strong
bargaining position to do so. Labour productivity (output per
man) in such industries is likely to be very high – partly because
of the skills of the workers employed but also because they are
fortunate enough to be working with large quantities of capital.
High wages can be justified on grounds of productivity and
employers are not averse to paying them, since wages form only
a small proportion of their total costs. Indeed it is vital for
managements to maintain industrial peace because of the enormous costs of allowing expensive plant to lie idle for any length
of time.

The danger is that production will become concentrated in a
relatively small number of very technologically sophisticated
plants – employing only a few highly paid workers. For the rest,
there is Professor Meade's vision of what he calls the Brave New
Capitalist's Paradise. 'Wage rates would thus be depressed; there
would have to be a large expansion of the production of the
labour-intensive goods and services which were in high demand
by the few multi-multi-millionaires; we would be back in a
super-world of an immiserized proletariat and of butlers, foot-
men, kitchen maids, and other hangers-on.'[6]

At a time when we have not yet been totally successful in
achieving continuous full employment, it may seem premature
to argue that it should no longer be regarded as a prime policy
objective. But in fact we are now sufficiently on top of the problem of creating work for all to concern ourselves also with questions of work for whom and where – and what sort of work?
The spread of employment, choice of jobs and the satisfaction
derived from work – all these lie behind the aggregate employment
statistics. And it is these real questions which have to be faced
up to – if people count.

6. J. E. Meade, *Efficiency, Equality of the Ownership of Property*, Allen
& Unwin, 1964, p. 33.

10

Behind the Growth Index

To put it mildly, it is no longer self-evident that maximizing the rate of economic growth is a proper objective of economic policy. In the past few decades, obsession with increasing output – long ago labelled by Colin Clark as 'growthmanship' – has been under attack on a number of fronts. Early doubts about the conventional enthusiasm for growth were expressed by J. K. Galbraith in his *Affluent Society*.[1] More recently, E. J. Mishan's *Cost of Economic Growth* has opened up fresh areas of debate. Galbraith was largely concerned with the distortions created by the growth process – seeing 'private affluence and public squalor' as its inevitable by-product. Mishan is even more caustic: 'There may be doubts amongst philosophers and heart-searching amongst poets, [but] to the multitude the kingdom of God is to be realized here, and now, on this earth; and it is to be realized via technological innovation, and at an exponential rate'.[2] Mishan's revulsion against 'growthmania' is total; for him, the answer to the question 'What conceivable alternative could there be to economic growth?' is obvious – we should contemplate the opposite policy of no-growth. Concerned about the depletion of global resources or sickened by the gross affluence of modern industrial societies, the conservationists and anti-materialists have been quick to join the bandwaggon. But there has also been a spirited defence of growth from those who argue that, although growth may create problems, increased output is also still the chief way of solving them. They further point out that the anti-growth mantle lies most easily on those who already enjoy substantial opulence and see their amenity threatened by its extension to the less fortunate.

1. Hamish Hamilton, 1958.
2. E. J. Mishan, *The Costs of Economic Growth*, p. 28.

But is this the right way to pose the question – as an issue of Growth versus No-growth? The terms of the debate are themselves highly suspect. It is the approach itself, single-minded concentration on the growth rate, which needs questioning – whether it is a matter of how to increase it *or* how to reduce it. Putting the issues in this framework conceals more real problems than it highlights. For the growth index is a very odd way of measuring anything (other than the increase in the total value of goods and services produced – which is what it is). Unfortunately, observers are seldom content to leave it at that. Such a heroic statistic as the growth in Gross National Product must, they feel, be of far-reaching significance. And so the process of interpretation begins. In no time at all, economic growth becomes synonymous with higher standards of living, economic progress and increases in economic welfare.

To see how misleading the growth index can be, consider the cautionary tale of a country which, at one time, used to pass under the name of Innocentia. Many years ago, life in Innocentia was simple – which is not to say idyllic, because, as economic historians are quick to remind us, the standard of living at that time was evidently far below that of today. The population was grouped into villages and small towns, and production consisted solely of basic goods – food, clothing and shelter. There was enough, and it was sufficiently well distributed, to provide everyone with primitive comfort. So far as we can tell, there was 'full employment' in the sense that all who wanted work could get it. But the Innocentians do not seem to have been a very industrious people: twenty hours was an average working week and a good many weeks were taken off for holidays and festivals. It has been estimated that the value of output (the G.N.P.) was then about £10,000 million a year.

What brought about the dramatic transformation of this primitive and backward society into the modern industrial state it is today was the invention and subsequent exploitation of a revolutionary new product – Candy Floss. Production first took place on the outskirts of a small northern township, and almost overnight Floss took Innocentia by storm. Demand seemed insatiable and all over the country firms sprang up producing a whole range of Floss products – natural, instant, dehydrated, frozen.

Naturally, these new enterprises were generally anxious to site themselves close to the market and this had far-reaching consequences for the Innocentian economy. Site values in the centres of towns and villages were bid up by the competing Floss producers, with the long-term result that workers, faced by a sharp rise in urban house prices, were gradually forced out into suburbia. This in turn involved new forms of expenditure – on roads and public and private transport to facilitate the journey to work and the movement of goods to final consumers.

Moreover, with more and more workers being absorbed by the new Floss enterprises and by the transport and communications sector, output per man in the traditional basic goods industries had to be considerably increased. One way in which this was achieved was to introduce a new forty-hour working week.

At this stage, some thirty years after the start of the economic revolution, the Innocentian G.N.P. had risen substantially:

	(£ m.)
Basic goods	10,000
Floss sector	10,000
Transport and communications	5,000
	25,000

Subsequent Innocentian development was landmarked by three major crises. Firstly, there was a point at which the Innocentians at long last seemed Floss-weary – it appeared that demand *had* finally been satiated. But the crisis was short-lived as enterprising Floss producers mounted massive advertising campaigns extolling the virtues of Floss consumption and also put a great deal of money into devising new Floss uses. Demand began to grow again as consumers turned to Floss fabrics, Floss cosmetics, Floss paints and a whole range of other startling and attractive new products.

A second setback was the revelation by expert medical opinion that Floss might be a prime cause of certain types of cancer which had been increasingly afflicting Innocentians. Once again, however, the pause in development was only temporary. Resources were poured into research into the precise causal relationship between Floss and cancer, and into the provision of hospitalization for those who continued to suffer.

Finally, as is inevitable in so sophisticated a society as Innocentia had become, there was an increase in social tensions. Sociologists are inclined to attribute the mounting crime rate in Innocentia to the rapid rate of change to which its people had been subjected, and to the undoubtedly hectic pace of life which its dramatic economic development had involved. Expenditure on police and prisons had to be sharply increased, and on the military as well – a defence against aggressive neighbours casting covetous eyes on Innocentian prosperity and know-how.

Today, Innocentia (or Avaricia as we now know it) is a very rich country indeed with one of the highest per capita income levels in the world. The extent of its remarkable development is shown by the increase in G.N.P. from an original £10,000 million to its present £60,000 million. Set out below is a simplified version of its 1972 national output statistics.

	(£ m.)
Basic goods	10,000
Floss	20,000
Transport, etc.	10,000
Sales promotion	5,000
Cancer research and hospitals	5,000
Police and prisons	3,000
Defence expenditure	7,000
Total G.N.P.	60,000

An economic miracle if ever there was one. However, Innocentian development is not without its critics. There are those, for example, who argue that its people are not really six times as well off as they were – which is what the figures suggest – because the working week is now twice as long as it used to be. That certainly seems a fair point. Then again, more puritanical protagonists question whether the introduction of Floss has really contributed to human welfare at all; what they would like to see is a reversion to the original state of happy, laughing Innocentians producing only basic goods. Obviously, this is a highly debatable matter which in the end is up to the Innocentians themselves – but a society without *any* Floss (or its equivalent) might be a very dull one which would not suit most of us.

What is most disturbing about the way in which the growth of Innocentian G.N.P. (or that of other modern industrial economies) is used as an indicator of increased material well-being is what goes into the statistics. Basic goods *plus* Floss only account for £30,000 million of total output. To a very large extent, the other half is made up of expenditure necessary to clean up the mess caused by growth of the Floss sector. It is spending which is an unfortunate and regrettable by-product of increased production, rather than output which is desired for itself.

Calculations of G.N.P. indiscriminately mix up 'goods' and 'bads' in this way to yield a grand total which therefore has very little meaning at all. To hail an increase in the rate of economic growth as a sign that we are doing well is patently nonsensical – unless we know whether the increased output is of 'goods' or 'bads'. Clearly, if economic growth is to be used to measure development, we must always ask – growth of *what*? Increased output of school buildings? Or Concordes? Or ear-muffs? Or aspirins? The answer is very relevant to whether or not we welcome economic growth, but it is a matter which is concealed rather than illuminated by the way in which gross national production figures are presented as a grand hotch-potch of both benefits and drawbacks.

An equally damaging line of criticism of G.N.P. calculations is to enquire about what they leave out. What goes in, since output is measured in terms of prices, is largely that part of output which is bought and sold. But a sizeable proportion of the total consumer satisfaction in an economy may in fact be derived from goods and services which are never 'marketed' in this obvious way. If I grow vegetables in my garden, for example, the result is clearly part of the national output, but not one on which a price is ever put. An even larger element of non-marketed services is the effort of housewives in cleaning, cooking and generally maintaining their homes. And thirdly, there is the 'output' of government social agencies – providing education, hospitals and other facilities for which in a welfare state the customer only partially pays.

To some degree, national income statisticians have overcome these problems. Governmental services *are* included in national income, but they are valued at cost, since there is no obvious price which can be set for them. The flow of satisfaction which an owner-occupier derives from his house is also taken into account, by 'imputing' a notional rent as a measure of that satisfaction. But there are times when national income figures are badly distorted by failure fully to allow for non-marketed elements in national output. During a war, for example, G.N.P. may be growing at a substantial rate. However, part of this growth may come from the increased employment of women who are forced in the process to have to relatively neglect their own homes. What is recorded in the statistics is their contribution to increased marketed output; what goes unrecorded is the reduction in the amount of housework which they are able to do. (Another reason for increased production during a war period may be that we are all working a good deal harder. But this increased human effort is, once again, something which the national income figures tell us nothing about.)

So far we have been talking only about *gross* national product. A related concept is that of *net* national product, which is the measure of the value of output after allowance has been made for replacing capital which has been worn out during the course of producing that output. Suppose for example, at the beginning of a year, an economy starts off with a stock of factories and machines of £1,000,000 million. At the end of the year it has produced a total output of, say, £40,000 million. But during the year the value of the original factories and machines has declined by £10,000 million. Then the *net* national product is £40,000 million *less* than £10,000 million depreciation of the capital stock. Net national product is the value of output produced while maintaining the value of its capital stock intact.

Numerous technical problems arise for the statisticians in determining the amount which should be deducted for depreciation. These need not concern us here. What should concern us is the narrow coverage of what is conventionally included in the capital stock calculation. Traditionally, capital refers to a stock of *physical* assets – plant, machinery, buildings, roads and suchlike. Since they embody scarce resources they have a price, and they can therefore – more or less – be measured.

However, estimating the capital stock of an economy in this way leaves out two very important elements. The first is the quantity of *human* capital which an economy has managed to build up over the years – the ability, aptitude, health, skills and tradition of its people without which no production is possible. Once again the wartime example is relevant. If national output is increased only at the expense of eroding human capital (by neglecting education, impairing health through overwork, etc.) then we really ought to deduct from gross output an appropriate 'human depreciation' figure before calculating net national product. Admittedly, this would be a difficult statistical exercise. But it sometimes makes more sense to hazard a guess about the relatively 'unquantifiable' than to spend a great deal of effort in refining the measurability of the quantifiable but less significant parts of the overall sum.

A second major omission from the national accounts is one which has been causing increasing concern of late. Economists, principally concerned with resources in finite supply, have traditionally identified a category of 'free goods' as being irrelevant to their particular study. Such goods – air, water (in certain circumstances) and land (in even more particular conditions) – have been labelled 'free' in the sense that they are in sufficiently abundant supply for all who want them to have as much as they like. They therefore create no economic problem.

What has been increasingly recognized in recent years is the extent to which the quantity and quality of these goods is affected by our present scale and processes of production. The problem of *pollution* is seen as more and more urgent and threatening. The fact that certain goods are 'free' means that firms and individuals have not been obliged to take them into account in their production and consumption decisions. That is because the costs which are involved are *external* – they fall on others. Thus the passing tourist who litters the countryside with his rubbish does so at no personal detriment because he is not coming that way again; but his action may mar the enjoyment of countless others – *they* bear the cost. Similarly, the ill-health, inconvenience and loss of amenity caused by a factory chimney belching smoke in the sky never appears in the company's accounts; it is, once again, an external cost borne by the community in the surrounding area.

The costs are nonetheless real. And they are of evermounting proportions. Air and water may be in abundance, but pure air and clean water are increasingly scarce resources. The social bill which has to be met as a result of the current scale of pollution is difficult to quantify but certainly enormous. What we ought to be doing is to subtract these social costs, this depreciation in our stock of *natural* capital, from the total of national output before arriving at the proper net figure.

Quite staggering estimates have been made, for example, about the costs of air pollution. The chief villains in this respect are power stations and the internal combustion engine. Dirty air helps to destroy not only vegetable life, property and property values but human beings as well. The Council for Environmental Quality has estimated that, taking into account the pollution of air alone, the United States gross national product should be reduced by over ten billion dollars a year. In fact, however, the standard method of G.N.P. calculation involves – as Barbara Ward points out – such irrationalities as 'making no subtraction for days lost or lungs congested' (as a result of air pollution) but 'includes doctors' earnings for putting the troubles right'.[3]

Precisely the same procedure is applied in the case of other pollutants – of water by the discharge of industrial and domestic effluents, of land by the indiscriminate use of pesticides. The original cost of creating the mess is neglected in national product accounts; but what does appear are the costs of cleaning it up. Those costs are then added on to other forms of output to yield

3. B. Ward and René Dubos, *Only One Earth*, Penguin Books, 1972, p. 104.

a grand G.N.P. total which is used as an index of economic progress.

None of this represents an attack on the desirability of economic growth. Rather it suggests that the growth versus anti-growth debate is couched in terms which themselves make meaningful discussion extremely difficult. Economic growth – which has been regarded as a major *end* of post-war economic policy – turns out, on closer scrutiny, to be an extraordinarily dubious objective. At best, it can be seen as a *means* to the achievement of aims which *are* significant. But in many ways it would be better if we were to forget about growth altogether and set up alternative indicators of economic progress which focus the real issues concealed by the growth index.

'Do we want more growth?' is a question which, after all, it is impossible to answer rationally without a good deal more specific information. We must know, first of all, growth of what? Goods or bads? The composition of output – and, in particular, how a proper balance can be struck between private and public goods – is a vital issue which is seldom brought to the forefront of popular debate. Secondly, we must ask 'Growth for whom?' To which elements in society do the benefits of increased output accrue? Partly, once again, this is a matter of which output is being increased. It also depends on what meanwhile is happening to the distribution of income and wealth. And, thirdly, what costs have been incurred in achieving economic growth? What has been the effect of increased growth on the environment, on amenity, on the pace and quality of working life and leisure?

These are all real world issues – which will be examined in more detail in later chapters – and they are hidden away in simplistic concentration on increasing growth as an objective in itself. Certainly, some types of growth *could* serve to solve problems which we all regard as 'urgent and menacing'. But growth can create 'diswelfare' as well as welfare. What above all we must get away from is the idea that growth automatically increases the living standards of the mass of people and the quality of their lives. That there is no such easy equation can be seen from the example of the United States – with a long-term growth performance matched by few other countries. The fact that U.S. output per head is perhaps twice as great as our own does not mean that the majority of American citizens enjoy a standard of living double that of their British counterparts. Behind the impressive economic statistics lies a society which combines the capacity to send men to the moon with the inability to cope with the problems of cities in which it is unsafe to venture out at night. The Great American Dream shows signs of degenerating into a fearful nightmare.

To repeat, the foolishness results from '*single-minded* concentration on *aggregate* production as a social goal'.[4] But how seriously should we take the more extreme view that *any* increased production is undesirable? Anti-materialism is generally the province of the 'haves' rather than the 'have-nots'. It is the middle class, appalled at the deterioration of foreign beaches resulting from package-tour holiday-makers, concerned at the congestion and pollution caused by the fact that so many others now enjoy the private motor car, who are most prone to admonish society in general on the evils of materialism. It is observers in the rich countries of the world who tend to extol the virtues of the simple life and urge on poor nations caution in creating a desire for material opulence. With the amount of basic poverty which today exists throughout the world, it is surely premature to deny the real benefits which are still to be derived from increased material well-being.

We still need increased output. But it must be of the right sort, directed towards solving the real underlying problems of our society and produced by a technology which is not blatantly wasteful of limited natural resources. These are matters to which we shall return in subsequent chapters.

4. Ward and Dubos, op. cit.

The Way of the Market

Chapter 2 outlined two general systems for deciding how our limited stocks of land, labour and capital can be used to best advantage. In a command economy, how much and what to produce, for whom and using which techniques are all administrative decisions taken by a planning authority. A market economy, on the other hand, leaves these matters to be determined by the forces of supply and demand, with relative *prices* signalling what the pattern of production and distribution should be.

It is difficult to think of real examples of either a pure command economy or a pure market economy. All in fact are mixed economies, combining elements of both systems. Obviously, the mix varies greatly between the Soviet Union, the United States, Cuba and the United Kingdom. But the difference is one of degree rather of kind, and it is a distinction which is becoming increasingly blurred. For example, the growing affluence of the Soviet Union has led the authorities to leave a growing proportion of total production to be determined by the price mechanism; that is partly because in an advanced economy the volume and complexity of production decisions becomes overwhelming, and partly because when output is increasingly made up of consumer goods it seems sensible to allow consumers to say what *they* want. In the United States, on the other hand, there is the opposite tendency for the administration to take over from the market. It is recognized that in areas like defence, lunar exploration, education and transport, the market outcome would, for various reasons, be unacceptable.

In this chapter and coming chapters we look more closely into the ways of the market system. How is it supposed to work ideally, and in what respects does it fall short of this ideal in practice? How far can it be relied upon to solve the problems of the real world?

To begin with, though, a restatement of the market mechanism in a world of textbook purity. We have already outlined its basic workings in Chapter 2 and seen what is claimed for it: that it is the most efficient way of deciding how resources (land, labour and capital) should be used to make sure that consumers get the best value they can for their money. In economists' jargon, it leads to an optimum allocation of resources.

Consumers, it is supposed, have wants far in excess of what their limited incomes can buy. They therefore have to choose. And if they do so calculatingly and rationally (and on the basis of full information about the alternatives available), they will finish up in a position of getting equal satisfaction from the last ten pence which they have spent on each of the products they buy. If that is not the case, it will pay them to substitute some goods for others until it is so. Only then will they be maximizing the satisfaction that can be derived from their incomes, and they will have done so by *marginal* calculations – asking, of each item of consumption, 'how much is this adding to my satisfaction and how much is it costing me?'

Firms are also assumed to be maximizers, but for them it is profits which are the spur. To make the greatest profit possible they too must act marginally. Some units of output would add more to their costs than to their total receipts; they therefore won't produce them. Others, adding more to revenue than costs, are profitable. The golden rule for profit maximization is: expand output to the point at which the last unit produced adds as much to revenue (marginal revenue) as it adds to costs (marginal cost). And similarly, when it comes to inputs, firms will maximize profits when, for example, the last man they take on adds as much to their total wage bill as their total receipts are increased by selling the larger output which results from his employment.

What brings them all into touch – consumers, firms and factors of production – are prices. Prices form the key element in the market system.

The price of anything depends on how much of it is offered for sale (supply) and the amount which people are prepared to buy (demand). The interests of consumers and producers are at odds with each other. Consumers want lower prices and producers try to charge as much as they can. For consumers, the lower the price, the greater generally is the quantity of a product which they are prepared to buy. A typical set of consumers' plans is shown in Fig. 26A – a demand curve showing that the higher

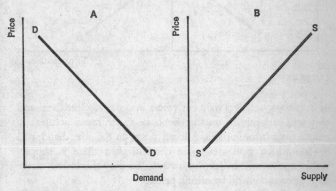

Figure 26

the price the less consumers would be willing to buy. Firms, on the other hand, react in the opposite way. The higher the price which *they* can get, the greater the quantity that they are prepared to put on the market. A simple production plan for an industry is illustrated graphically in the supply curve of Fig. 26B.

The demand and supply curves show just *plans*. They indicate what consumers and firms *would* do if the price were such and such. But how is the actual market price determined? Fig. 27 brings together the two sets of information about demand and supply plans. Quite clearly there is only one price at which plans to produce and plans to consume are compatible. This so-called 'equilibrium' price is the one towards which market forces will always be pressing. If price is higher than that, the amount supplied will exceed the amount demanded. Stocks will pile up

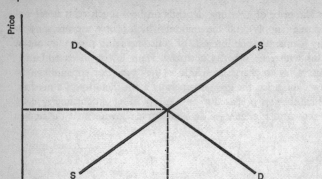

Figure 27

in the shops; retailers may cut prices in order to clear them and they will certainly be on the telephone to the manufacturers to reduce their future orders. A lower price, on the other hand, will be one which generates more demand than there is supply. Either queues will be formed, or retailers may themselves choke off the excess demand by raising prices.

In the ideal market system it is the consumer who calls the tune. Suppose, for example, that there is a switch in taste away

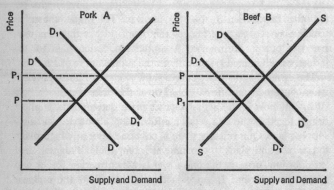

Figure 28

from beef and in favour of pork. Fig. 28 shows the effect on their relative prices. The increased popularity of pork means that housewives are willing to buy more of it than previously at any given price. In other words (Fig. 28A), the demand curve shifts bodily to the right $(D_1 D_1)$. The upshot is that equilibrium price of pork rices from P to P1, and this induces farmers to produce the extra quantity now demanded. Similarly, as Fig. 28B shows, the effect of the reduced popularity of beef is that its demand curve moves to the left $(D_1 D_1)$ as consumers are now prepared to buy only smaller amounts at any given price. Equilibrium price fall from P to P_1 – and supply is consequently choked off.

In this way, prices act as a link between consumers and resources. Higher demand by consumers for a particular product will force up its price. The firms getting greater revenue as a result will be able to bid resources – land, labour and capital – away from other firms whose products are less popular. The consumer, despite having no direct contact with factors of production, has nonetheless dictated the way in which they are deployed. The consumer is sovereign. Prices, reflecting consumer demands *and* the relative scarcity of resources in an economy, act as signposts pointing to the way in which those resources should be allocated.

The ideal market system is one in which well-informed consumers make careful and rational choices; producers charge prices enough only to cover costs plus a 'normal' profit just sufficient to keep them in business; and resources can be moved freely from one type of production to another in response to changing consumer demands. Provided that all these conditions are met, the outcome will be an optimum use of resources with consumers being satisfied to the greatest possible extent.

This is the mesmeric appeal of the price mechanism. It allocates resources optimally. And it is beautifully simple. All that is needed is that we be ourselves and pursue our own self-interest. Magically, without any intervention from the authorities, resources are channelled into their most efficient uses.

But does it work in practice? We have already examined one glaring defect: the unlikelihood that an unregulated market economy will yield stable full employment. But does it, in the real world, even guarantee that those resources which *are* employed are used efficiently? There are many grounds for doubt.

If their satisfactions are to be maximized, consumers must act like 'economic men' – coldly calculating, rational and perfectly knowledgeable. Are they really like this, or are they subject to habit and impulse, ignorant of the prices and qualities of goods offered for sale, and easily manipulated and deceived by advertising? Even if consumers as a whole are sovereign, the highly unequal distribution of income and wealth certainly means that some are more sovereign than others; the price mechanism cannot distinguish between a pound spent by a poor man and a pound spent by a rich man, although they may mean very different things.

Then again, it can be argued that consumers are *not*, in practice, sovereign. Firms do not passively respond to their demands, but set out deliberately to mould consumer tastes so that supply creates demand rather than the other way round. The role of profits is a further case where practice may seriously diverge from the ideal. Profits ought to be indicators of efficiency – 'the index of what people want. Where high profits are being made, there is unsatisfied demand and the high profits will attract more capital and more energy into meeting it. Where low profits are being made, capital and energy are being wasted.' [1] But in reality high profits can also arise because firms have achieved a dominant market position in which they can charge high prices with impunity: profits in this case reflect the degree of monopoly rather than competitive efficiency.

Finally, resources in practice are not, as the theory assumes, perfectly mobile. Workers and capital do not move quickly and freely from one line of production to another in response to price signals. And even when market forces do work, they may do so very slowly. A particular industry may be bound to decline in face of falling demand, but its contraction may be long drawn out and painful.

These are all matters which we shall be examining later in the real context of the British economy. But if there is anything in

1. E. Powell, *Freedom and Reality*, Batsford, 1969, p. 28.

these criticisms of the market economy, then prices are not very reliable or effective signals for allocating resources. The *practical* limitations of the market provide a rationale for government intervention aimed at creating the necessary conditions to make the price mechanism work as it should ideally (for example, by anti-monopoly legislation) or anticipating the outcome of market forces and speeding them up.

So far, we are still assuming that the market system is an appropriate *ideal* which would be acceptable if only its blemishes and imperfections could be removed. But even this way of looking at it is very questionable.

(1) A basic criticism of the market system concerns what is *omitted* from the price calculus. Firms will produce only if their revenue is at least equal to their costs (including an appropriate return to capital). Revenue in excess of costs may induce them to expand production. Revenue below costs will be a sign that they should contract and perhaps ultimately leave an industry altogether under the 'discipline of the market'. All these calculations are naturally internal to the firm. What goes into its balance sheet are the costs and the benefits as they appear to that individual production unit.

However, economists have long recognized that these may not represent the whole story. In the course of its production, a firm may bestow on other producers incidental benefits which do not show up in its own balance sheet. And it may impose costs on the economy which it does not itself have to bear. These external or social costs and benefits – genuinely economic though they are – may not be reflected at all in actual market prices which determine the way in which resources are allocated.

We have become increasingly aware of the degree to which private and social costs and benefits may diverge. Closing down a coalmine in a Scottish village may be perfectly justifiable on the *commercial* grounds that it simply does not pay. But, *economically*, keeping the pit open may be justifiable if the resources involved are highly specific and immobile, so that releasing them from their present use does not mean that they are redeployed in more efficient lines of production. For most people, the criterion of whether something pays is the economic be-all-

and-end-all. In fact, it is important that wider costs and benefits are taken into account in determining economic viability.

(2) A further limitation of the market system is that it may lead to the production of goods generally regarded as undesirable, while at the same time failing to produce goods which are not easily priced. A free market could, for example, lead to the output of hard drugs in response to consumer demands. On the other hand, leaving matters like defence or education to the market is not likely to work very well. Defence must be provided collectively because it is impossible for the market to discriminate between those who would be prepared to pay and those who would not; both would be defended regardless. And social services cannot be left to the market because they are 'merit' goods – those which we decide *ought* to be provided on a scale perhaps greater than that which people would be prepared to pay for privately.

(3) The market mechanism may work in a way which most people would regard as 'unfair'. It can be argued that 'The only point about price, the only usefulness about price, is to indicate the relationship of supply and demand. There is no justice or injustice about it, any more than about the readings on a thermometer or a pressure gauge.'[2] But prices are based on the existing income distribution which many would regard as unsatisfactory, and the operation of the market mechanism perpetuates inequalities which, as will be argued later, have little economic or moral justification.

(4) Finally, there are those who would condemn the market system at a philosophical level as being based on uncurbed individualism and exploiting the meaner of human motives.

Certainly, it is in this last very broad framework that discussion about the pros and cons of the market economy are frequently couched. The market mechanism is equated with capitalist free enterprise; the alternative is seen as socialist planning. But is this the real issue?

We must distinguish between the market mechanism as an instrument and as a philosophy. As an instrument, its critics point to its past associations and practical outcome. But these

2. Powell, op. cit., p. 28.

are not intrinsic to the use of prices in allocating resources. The fact that it has been more commonly used in capitalist economies does not mean that it would have no place in a society in which the means of production were publicly owned. It may in the past have led to inequality, instability and an unacceptable pattern of output. But it could be used to achieve quite different results. Planning need not be a stark alternative to the market system. It can help to make it work more effectively.

Writers of the extreme left sometimes talk of the market system ultimately withering away with the transition to socialism. For them, the market is more than an instrument. It is the expression of a political philosophy. But until we devise some clear alternative techniques for coping with the enormously complex problems of allocating resources in a modern industrial economy such a view remains utopian. Meanwhile we should concentrate on making the market system work as we want it to, which involves not only creating conditions in which it can function at its neutral best but also building into it whatever values we think important.

In the next chapters we look first at the actual institutional framework in which market forces currently work. We must then decide what it is that we want from the economy. And then we can see what the policy implications are if the market is to be the means of bringing about a more acceptable economic and social outcome.

12

What's Left of Consumer Sovereignty?

The notion of consumer sovereignty is the very heart of the theory of the market economy. In its idealized form, it is the consumers who hold the initiative. The whole economic system is geared to meeting their demands to the fullest possible extent, with firms responding to their changing wants as transmitted through the signals of the price mechanism. But *is* the consumer in fact king in the real world of the 1970s? Or are the facts of the matter so at variance with the postulates of the model that consumer sovereignty is now a myth?

There are those who see no divergence between ideal and reality. For Enoch Powell, for example, free enterprise is sufficient to guarantee that the consumer will continue to dominate the centre of the stage.

The free enterprise economy is the true counterpart of democracy: it is the only system which gives everyone a say. Everyone who goes into a shop and chooses one article rather than another is casting a vote in the economic ballot box: with thousands or millions of others that choice is signalled to production and investment and helps to mould the world just a tiny fraction nearer to people's desire. In this great and continuous general election of the free economy nobody, not even the poorest, is disenfranchised: we are all voting all the time. Socialism is designed on the opposite pattern: it is designed to prevent people getting their own way, otherwise there would be no point in it.[1]

But for others, the traditional economic theory of consumer behaviour is no more than a faded snapshot of the way things may have been a century ago. Today, they argue, far from pulling the strings, it is the consumers themselves who are the puppets.

To get to the truth of the matter we must look first at the

1. E. Powell, *Freedom and Reality*, p. 33.

consumer himself and ask how closely he resembles the economic man of traditional theory.

Clearly we are not all as rational, consistent and precisely calculating as consumers are in the textbooks. But then the theory never purported to be a straightforward description of reality; it was intended as a highly stylized account of what actually happened. Provided that a fair proportion of consumers act very broadly in the way in which the theory suggests, the fact that the rest of us are careless, irrational and inconsistent need not affect the issue. Given that a good deal of consumption is undertaken by housewives on behalf of the family unit, the theoretical assumptions about consumers do not seem far wrong; a large number of buyers *are* very much aware of what is on offer, do shop around to get the best value they can for their money.

But, however much they take the trouble, it is increasingly difficult for consumers in the real world to meet another requirement of the theoretical model: that they should be perfectly knowledgeable about what they are buying. In an affluent society an increasing proportion of incomes is spent on expensive consumer durable goods like cars, washing machines, televisions, refrigerators and tape recorders. These are all technologically very sophisticated products about which it is difficult to be well-informed. Most people simply lack the technical knowledge to be able to decide rationally whether one brand of a product is a better or worse buy than another. The Consumers Association provides a regular flow of information through *Which*? and its associated journals, but only to a limited clientele – who may, incidentally, be those who are already relatively well-informed and least in need of it.

To make matters worse, these complex consumer durables are major items of expenditure which recur only at infrequent intervals. Buy a tin of soup which you discover to be tasteless and you can transfer to another brand at once. But by the time the car which has been continuously unsatisfactory becomes due for replacement the model has been succeeded by another about which we are as ignorant as we were about its predecessor.

Another gap between theory and reality emerges when we look

at the consumer in his relations with others. Theory investigates the behaviour of the consumer in isolation; in principle, the consumer could be shut up in a room on his own and draw up a list of his wants in order of preference. In fact consumption takes place in a social context. What consumers want depends partly on what other consumers already have or are thinking of getting. We must keep up with the Joneses or, better still, be one step ahead of them. This is what economists term the 'demonstration effect'. And on top of this is purely conspicuous consumption: goods bought, not so much for the satisfaction of using them, but because they are useful indicators of social status.

This interdependence of consumption decisions, although it renders a good deal of traditional theory irrelevant, is not in itself a limitation on consumer sovereignty in the same way that consumer ignorance is. But they both make it easier for sovereignty to be eroded from another quarter. Ignorance, vanity and envy all help to make the consuming public very susceptible to manipulation by producers. In theory, firms are passive agents waiting for consumer demands to come through the pipeline. In practice, what is to stop them *creating* demands which they can then profitably satisfy? Does demand create supply in the real world according to what Galbraith calls 'the accepted sequence'?[2] Or do giant companies now impose a 'revised sequence' in which supply creates its own demand? They certainly have both the motive and the means to do so.

First, the motive. Modern industrial production is technologically highly complex and involves massive capital outlays on research, pilot projects and the tooling-up of factories. The cost can be recouped only if these enormous overheads can be spread over a very large volume of sales. Given these technological imperatives, argues Galbraith, giant firms simply cannot afford to introduce a product just hoping that the demand will be there on the off chance that it may be a success. 'Technology, with its companion commitment of time and capital, means that the needs of consumers must be anticipated – by months or

2. J. K. Galbraith, *The New Industrial State*, Penguin Books, 1969, pp. 216–17.

years. When the distant day arrives the consumer's willingness to buy may well be lacking ... The needed action ... is evident: in addition to deciding what the consumer will want and will pay, the firm must take every feasible step to see that what it decides to produce is wanted by the consumer at a remunerative price.' [3] They must *create* a market and be as sure as possible that consumers *will* be receptive to their new product. With the degree of advanced commitment which modern technological processes involve firms find it far too risky 'to rely on the untutored responses of the consumer'.[4]

Nor need they do so, for the means of reducing the uncertainties of the market are at hand. Advertising, sales promotion, market research and public relations are now all highly developed techniques. Their effectiveness has been greatly increased by the advent of commercial broadcasting. Big business in themselves, advertising and sales promotion account for nearly 3 per cent of the gross national product. What is left of consumer sovereignty under continuous bombardment from the marketing men?

In some ways advertising is positively beneficial to consumer interests. Some advertising is almost wholly informative and all advertising involves the transmission of *some* information. To this extent, consumer knowledge of alternatives is increased and he can make more rational choices. Classified advertisements – like the small ads in the newspapers – account for nearly 20 per cent of total spending in this field; clearly most of these serve a perfectly useful function of bringing buyers and sellers together. On the other hand, a good deal of large-scale advertising contains extraordinarily little hard fact. It chiefly consists of emphasizing the name of the company and extolling the virtues of the product in the most general terms; looking back at the advertisements of by-gone days suggests that the informative content of advertising has markedly diminished.

But advertising and other marketing techniques also seek to persuade. In this role they can erode consumer sovereignty in a variety of ways. The consumer may, for example, be deceived by advertising. Trouble is in store for advertisers who deliberately falsify the facts. But there is no law to stop them suggesting that

3. Galbraith, op. cit., p. 33.   4. ibid., p. 34.

some actually minor product difference is a major reason why consumers should buy Brand X rather than Brand Y. The customer may be seduced by advertising into impulse buys which he later regrets. And he may be lured into an initial purchase of a product the consumption of which subsequently becomes habitual, so that his future range of choice is limited: cigarette smoking is the obvious example.

However, the major charge against modern marketing methods is that they work not so much to enable producers to respond to consumers' *given* wants as actually to engender new wants. It is the producer tail which wags the consumer dog. There is a lot in this, although the case rests on a rather uneasy distinction between 'spontaneous' wants, which somehow reside in the consumer himself, and 'manipulated' wants, which are artificially created by sales promotion. It is not easy to identify the difference in practice because, as A. P. Lerner has put it, 'In a rich society like ours, only a very tiny part of what people want is determined by their physical and chemical make-up. Almost all their needs and desires are built on observation and imitation.'[5]

Product innovation is continually opening up new prospects which consumers previously did not know were even technically feasible. Before television was invented people did not demand moving pictures in their homes because there was no point in them doing so. But once television became available, consumer demand built up rapidly. Had producers created a new want? Or had they merely satisfied the *latent* desires of consumers?

It is possible to find some supporting evidence for this latter view in the fact that firms spend large sums in investigating the potential demand for their products before launching them. 'Available studies indicate that most products that product-development departments regard as "technically successful developments" are never launched on the market because of negative results in market research and market tests.'[6] Producers, it

5. A. P. Lerner, 'The Economics and Politics of Consumer Sovereignty', *American Economic Review Papers and Proceedings*, May 1972, p. 258.

6. A. Lindbeck, *The Political Economy of the New Left. An Outsider's View*, Harper & Row, 1971, p. 43.

seems, do still take into account what their customers want. And consumers can always say no. 'The scanty evidence available suggests that a very large fraction of the products that are actually launched on markets fail, despite often extensive advance market studies. A rather usual comment in the literature is that between one-third and one-half of all products put on the market are considered failures by the sponsoring firms, in the sense that they withdraw the product from the market within one year.'[7]

However, this view that producers use modern marketing techniques simply to react more sensitively to consumers' own desires ignores the extent to which consumers are already prisoners of the commercial environment dominated by giant industrial companies. The consumer is himself the product of an ethos in which he has been encouraged to aim at the acquisition of ever greater quantities of goods and services. And within this general pressure towards greater consumption firms then compete by working on the *weaknesses* of consumers: the fact that they *are* more responsive to irrational persuasion than hard information, and that their vanity, envy and insecurity make them easy and willing victims of manipulation. It is the big industrial producers who set the pace, and the result is a far cry from the economist's simple model of consumer behaviour, in which, generally, the theory is described in terms of 'commodities – bread, tea, oranges, salt, sugar – which are produced outside the industrial system or for which the management of demand is peculiarly difficult'.[8]

Moreover, the range of options open to the consumer in exercising his choice is largely determined by producers. It is they who select the candidates for whom consumers are free to vote and over the years the candidates have come to look more and more alike, of inferior quality and shorter-lived. We are free to choose between alternative brands of mass-produced bread, but it is getting more difficult to opt for bread freshly baked in a local bakery. In food shops it is increasingly the case that the only difference between the manufacturer's product and the retailer's 'own brand' is in the packaging. Consumption patterns

7. ibid.   8. Galbraith, op. cit., p. 220.

are biased towards goods most susceptible to mass production and marketing. Differentiation takes frivolous and wasteful forms – minor variations in car body designs to make last year's model obviously out of date, unnecessarily expensive packaging variations, trading stamps and 'free gifts'. Then again, there is the growing tendency to produce goods with built-in obsolescence. It is not that modern production techniques rule out products which will last. It is simply that it is not a paying proposition for manufacturers looking for regular replacement orders.

The extreme view that consumer sovereignty has been totally usurped is exaggerated. But certainly there has been a major shift to producer power since economists first elaborated their theory of the market in which the consumer always held the initiative. The practice is very far from that ideal. But how far anyway is the ideal itself an acceptable one? *Should* the consumer be sovereign?

This is a delicate question involving issues of individual liberty. The notion that the State should intervene to say that people *ought* to consume less of some goods and more of others easily conjures up the spectre of totalitarian dreariness. But surely there would be few who would argue that if there was a substantial demand for hard drugs then it should be met commercially. Similarly, there is general agreement that matters like education and health are too important for individuals to be left entirely free to decide how much they will spend on them. In other words we deliberately limit consumer sovereignty to achieve certain *social* goals.

Or consider another example – that of car safety. Suppose that the majority of consumers express a preference for low-priced cars rather than more expensive models incorporating seat belts and safety design. It might be arguable whether or not the State should intervene to protect them against themselves. But it certainly has an obligation to safeguard the interests of other road users.

This raises much more general issues. Individual consumption decisions cannot be examined in isolation. We must also be concerned with their collective outcome. For example, consumers of noisy jet air transport affect other consumers – of housing situated near our major airports. The sovereignty of particular groups of consumers may have to be curtailed in order that consumers as a whole are best satisfied. Again, the market mechanism has a basic bias towards private rather than public consumption. It is much easier for manufacturers to persuade their customers that they will be happier as a result of having bought their products than it is for governments to induce taxpayers to finance services and amenities from which all, rather than just they themselves, will benefit. And sometimes private and public consumption decisions are complementary. More cars means more roads, but car users, suffering from the congestion caused by other car users, still oppose the increased taxes which might go to provide them. There is no mechanism by which individuals can see the car/road package as a whole and take rational decisions in choosing between more private or more public transport.

These are all matters of what should be the proper composition of output – the subject of Chapter 17. How satisfied can we be with an economic system which can ignore the *needs* of those lacking adequate shelter, food and warmth while at the same time satisfying the *wants* for vaginal deodorants, electric toothbrushes and quadraphonic sound?

To a large extent these imbalances are caused by the fact that some consumers are clearly a great deal more sovereign than others. In our 'economic democracy' some have many more votes than others, and it is to their demands that production is therefore geared. Prices, on which the market mechanism is based, reflect any underlying disparities in income and wealth; change that, and the strength of demand for various goods would also alter, relative prices would be readjusted and a quite different pattern of production would emerge. We shall be looking in Chapters 14–16 at the facts and theories of income distribution.

Before that, however, we should see what light economics throws on the cause of eroded consumer sovereignty – the growth of producer power.

13

The Firm in Theory and Practice

The ability of a market economy to allocate resources efficiently depends on the existence of free competition. Much of the theory of the market system is therefore devoted to spelling out the properties of free competition and the dangers of diverging from it. What we question in this chapter is whether the traditional theory of the firm bears any relation to what in fact goes on in the real world.

The textbook picture of the firm is of a single-plant, single-product enterprise run by single-minded 'entrepreneurs' with the sole object in life of maximizing profits. The theory then portrays firms such as these in a variety of industrial settings. The first is that of perfect competition, a situation with two main features. There are a large number of buyers and sellers each too small independently to influence the market price. And there is free entry into the industry. In perfect competition, the firm is said to be a price-taker.

To see what is meant by this, take the case of a market gardener in, say, Bedfordshire (and also suppose that there are no such things as Marketing Boards). Early each morning, a lorry from a local haulage firm calls to take his lettuces for sale at Covent Garden. The producer does not tell the lorry driver how much he wants for the lettuces; it is left to him to get the best price he can. The price which he *does* get depends entirely on the situation in Covent Garden on any particular day. There, lettuces will be coming in from a large number of different sources, and they will be bought by many independent wholesalers, hotels and so on. The actual market price on that day will be one which balances supply and demand. Suppose, for example, that it settles at 3p per lettuce. Then, if the market gardener had instructed the lorry driver to accept no less than 4p, he would have sold none, because one lettuce is much like another and nobody would have bought his more expensive produce. On the other hand, he would have been foolish to ask for only 2p when the going rate turned out to be 3p. The best he can do is to take what the market offers.

The great theoretical attraction of the perfectly competitive combination of price-taking and free entry is that it yields an outcome in which prices and profits are pushed down to minimum levels. If profits happen temporarily to rise above 'normal' level (defined as that which is just sufficient to keep firms in their present line of business) then the result will be that new firms are attracted into the industry. The consequent increase in supply coming onto the market depresses price and eliminates the excess profits of the original group of producers.

This is the reason why the perfectly competitive model has retained such an appeal for economists for the century and a half since it was first formulated. Indeed, at that time it could be said to have roughly fitted the facts of the British economy, consisting as it did mostly of small owner-enterprises. The enormous structural changes which have subsequently taken place in the economy have rendered the model largely useless as a description of reality. But economic theorists, aware of this, have nonetheless continued to view perfect competition as the yardstick for measuring deviations from the ideal.

Thus, in a typical textbook of the pre-1930 vintage, lengthy discussion of the merits of perfect competition would be followed by the entry of the villain – monopoly, or the absence of competition. Monopoly occurred when the output of a good was completely dominated by a single producer. In this case, the firm *was* the industry. The effect, as could be shown by intricate geometrical diagrams, was that the monopolist – by restricting output and raising prices – could earn abnormal profits over and above those necessary to keep him in business. Moreover, it was claimed that monopolies, lacking a competitive stimulus, tended to be inefficient in other ways. They lacked the incentive to innovate and management became sluggish.

However, instances of monopoly – in the sense of complete absence of competition – are as difficult to find as perfect competition. During the 1930s, therefore, an attempt to add realism to the theory was made by the introduction of a new concept – 'monopolistic competition', or 'imperfect competition' as it became known, which was neither monopoly or competition but combined elements of both. Most firms, it was argued, although competing with many others, did so primarily through advertising and other forms of product differentiation. Shirt producers, for example, each would be trying to give his product a distinctive design, fashion or packaging which would attract consumer loyalty. To begin with, the firms in such an industry might make excess profits, but new firms would then set up in business and whittle them away. However, in the process excess capacity would be created in the original firms as they now had to share the market with a greater number of rivals. This tendency to chronic excess capacity is one of the main predictions of imperfect competition analysis – and something akin to it can perhaps be seen in the retail trade.

The extension of the theory of the firm to accommodate problems of imperfect competition was nonetheless very much within the traditional analytical framework. The firms' single-minded pursuit of profit-maximization was still assumed. And it still allowed the individual firm to be studied in isolation from others. This was possible because, under conditions of perfect and imperfect competition, each firm was too small for its activities to have any noticeable effect on the price and output decisions of others; nor, in turn, was it influenced by any other firm's policies. And in monopoly, effects on rivals could of course be ignored because there were no rivals.

But just how great a step towards realism did the new analysis represent? More broadly, how well can the traditional theory of the firm as a whole explain what happens in the real world?

In a modern industrial economy isolated instances can be found which do roughly approximate to perfect competition or monopoly. And the majority of firms probably operate in situations rather like imperfect competition. So far so good. But a substantial and growing proportion of output, and the bulk of industrial production, comes from firms in industries which can be classified under none of these headings. Undoubtedly, the most important market situation today is that of oligopoly. Olig-opoly is competition between the few – and the few are typically very large-scale enterprises who between them dominate an industry.

It is at just this point that traditional economic theory becomes least helpful. It offers very little indeed by way of explanation of oligopolistic behaviour. The principal reason for its failure to throw any light on the matter is the methodology of analysing a firm in isolation from others, which works in the cases of perfect and imperfect competition and monopoly but which completely breaks down in the case of oligopoly. That is because, when there are only a few large rivals in an industry, the *essence* of the prob-lem is their uncertainty about rivals' reactions to their own poli-cies. Oligopoly is above all featured by interdependence of rivals' pricing and output decisions. The biggest question mark for Firm X, contemplating a price rise for its product, is how Firms Y and Z will react. Will they just match the price increase, raise prices by a smaller amount, keep their prices the same or lower prices? Without this information, which is not available, Firm X cannot predict what its sales will be at the higher price. And, if it goes ahead with its price rise, Firm X in turn will have to decide how to respond to the reactions of Firms Y and Z.

It is precisely these dynamics of interdependence which tradi-tional theory is unable to handle. Attempts have been made to make the analysis of oligopolistic situations more manageable by making assumptions about rivals' reactions. Some early theorists even went so far as to assume that rivals would not react at all. That certainly enabled them to formulate determinate conclu-sions about oligopolistic pricing and output policies, but only, of course, at the cost of assuming away the oligopolistic problem itself! Others have argued that reactions will be asymmetrical – that price rises will not be followed by rivals, whereas price cuts will. This, they suggest, makes for price stability in oligopolistic situations, with competition diverted to product differentiation, innovation and general service competition. Others again have sought an explanation of oligopolistic behaviour by postulating price leadership or evolving complex strategical options based on the mathematical theory of games.

One leading economist warns his student readers that a standard textbook on oligopoly theory 'will give him an impression of the complexity of the problem. But if, when he has finished his study, he asks himself what he can predict about oligopolistic behaviour in the real world he will probably answer "little" or "nothing at all".'[1] In other words, we simply don't know how to explain the most important part of a modern industrial economy.

Nearly every major industry today – cars, oil, chemicals, tobacco, electricals – is dominated by a handful of giant companies. In Britain the largest hundred firms account for over half of all profits and employ about a third of the total industrial and commercial work-force. And the process of industrial concentration continues to accelerate. Spending on take-overs during the first half of the sixties was something like ten times that of the fifties. From a total of £550 million in 1966 it rose dramatically to some £1,600 million in 1968 and then to a new peak of over £2,500 million in 1972. Moreover, take-overs and mergers are frequently between already massive enterprises – Thorn–Radio Rentals, B.M.C.–Leyland, Unilever–Allied Breweries, Boots–Timothy Whites, A.E.I.–G.E.C., Imperial Tobacco–Courage. One estimate is that the mergers movement during the 1960s must have involved the transfer of some 20 per cent of the total net assets of manufacturing industry.

What lies behind this concentration of industry into larger and larger enterprises? The stock answer of economists and of the businesses themselves is that size is a necessary condition for achieving what are called economies of large-scale production. In many industries, higher production levels allow substantial cuts to be made in unit costs. Thus a 1962 estimated capital cost of a plant to produce 100,000 tons of iron a year worked out at £12.10 per ton, which would be slashed to only £5.60 a ton for a one-million-ton plant.[2] In the motor-car industry, 'Something like a 40 per cent reduction in costs can be expected as produc-

1. R. G. Lipsey, *Introduction to Positive Economics*, 2nd edn, Weidenfeld & Nicolson, 1963, p. 344.
2. C. Pratten and R. N. Dean, *The Economics of Large Scale Production in British Industry*, University of Cambridge Dept of Applied Economics Occasional Paper No. 3.

tion increases from 1,000 to 50,000 units per annum. Doubling volume to 100,000 units should lower costs by 15 per cent; while a further doubling to 200,000 should achieve another 10 per cent in savings. The jump to 400,000 yields an additional 5 per cent, and expansion beyond this point results in progressively smaller savings for each additional 100,000, the gains tapering off at a level of about 1,000,000.'[3] 'The Boeing 747 (Jumbo Jet) airliner, which is about two and a half times the size of the 707 airliner and carries about 390 passengers compared with about 140, is said to be 20–30 per cent cheaper in terms of direct operating costs per passenger.'[4]

All of these are examples of technical economies of scale. The large firm, because it can spread its overheads over a long production run, can often use superior techniques to its smaller rival, or achieve economies by installing a larger version of the same techniques, or combine techniques in a more efficient way. But in addition to technical economies there, are a number of other advantages accruing to a large firm.

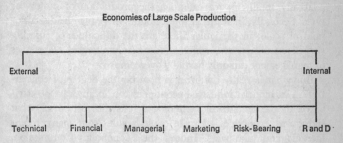

Figure 29

External economies are those which a firm enjoys because of the growth of an industry – the fact, for example, that it will pay other firms to set up to provide it with component parts or use its waste products as a raw material. Financially, the large firm may have access to sources like the Stock Exchange not available to

3. G. Maxcy and A. Silbertson, *The Motor Industry*, Allen & Unwin, 1959, p. 93.

4. G. Bannock, *The Juggernauts*, Weidenfeld & Nicolson, 1971, p. 113.

the small firm, and it may be able to borrow at lower rates. Managerial economies arise with specialization at the boardroom level and the employment of expertise and management aids like computers. On the marketing side, the large firm may be able to control its own distribution network and use mass media advertising to a greater extent. And through diversification it can spread its risks over a wide range of products.

All of these are essentially static advantages. But on top of these there is an important dynamic economy of scale in that the larger enterprise is able to devote a greater amount to research and development – from which, it hopes, new products and processes will emerge. In other words, the large firm not only holds all the aces now; it is also in a better position to develop in the future.

There is no denying the very real significance of economies of scale. On the other hand, it is easy to exaggerate them. First of all, advantages of size differ from industry to industry. The optimum size of plant may be large in the motor-car industry but relatively small, in, for example, the production of motor-car tyres. Secondly, in addition to economies there may be diseconomies of scale; in particular there are the difficulties of running very large enterprises, which modern computerized techniques of management can only partially overcome .

But what is really doubtful is how far the degree of concentration in modern industrial economies can in any case be attributed to the dictates of technology. It is difficult to see what significant economies of scale could result from many recent mergers and take-overs. Indeed the Monopolies Commission, since it was given powers to investigate them, has on occasions rejected prospective mergers on just this ground. Then again, particularly in the case of technical economies, it is the size of *plant* rather than the size of firm which counts. And yet many very large companies have made very little apparent effort to consolidate their production into fewer factories. Furthermore, much growth of firms has taken place through the acquisition of firms engaged in quite different lines of business; no very obvious economies result, for example, from a cigarette manufacturer taking over a potato-crisp producer.

Also remarkable is the fact that profitability, far from increasing, frequently declines with the size of the firm.[5] If that is so, and if it is also true that most of the present industrial giants have grown to a point far beyond any technological imperatives, then clearly we must ask some fundamental questions about what makes them tick.

Economic theory assumes that firms are profit-maximizers and that profits are an index of efficiency leading to movements of capital from one line of production to another. Both these propositions are questionable.

The Profit Motive. Doubt about whether firms are solely motivated by profit maximization stems principally from their changed institutional nature, first charted in the nineteen-thirties by Berle and Means and James Burnham.[6] Nearly all major firms and joint-stock companies are owned by shareholders but run by a board of directors. This divorce of ownership from control means that managerial and owner interests may not entirely coincide. Shareholders, no doubt, *are* solely interested in maximizing profits. But, because of their number, passiveness and lack of knowledge of the complex day-to-day operations of a giant corporation, they are in no position to *know* whether profits are being maximized or not.

None of this is to argue that private firms have lost interest in profits. But there may be a difference between maintaining a high and 'satisfactory' level of profits (enough to keep shareholders quiet and to provide capital for further expansion) and *maximizing* them. It is here that other motivations can be inserted. But what might they be?

Writers like Marris and Galbraith[7] emphasize that it is the managers or 'technostructure' who dominate the boards of large

5. J. M. Samels and D. Smyth, *Economica*, May 1968.
6. A. A. Berle and G. C. Means, *The Modern Corporation and Private prosperity*, New York, 1933; and J. Burnham, *The Managerial Revolution*, New York, 1941.
7. R. Marris, *The Economic Theory of Managerial Capitalism*, Macmillan, 1964; and J. K. Galbraith, *The New Industrial State*, Penguin Books, 1969.

companies rather than owners or owner nominees. Not themselves being profit earners, what they may be more concerned with are matters of respectability, status and security. Thus growth of the firm and its diversification into a range of different industries is important for a number of reasons. It enables the firm to achieve a dominant market position in which it is no longer threatened by competition. Its size enhances the status of the managers themselves. Its multiplicity of activities ensures its long-term survival as an ongoing permanent institution. And size can, for the corporation man, become an end in itself.

For Galbraith in particular, what this amounts to is that capitalism today has become a very different animal. The technostructure into whose hands control has largely passed is not only amenable to influence from the State: it positively welcomes it. No longer is there a conflict between State and private industry, because both aim at reducing future uncertainties through planning.

But has the leopard really changed its spots? Certainly the emergence of a powerful managerial class makes it possible to inject motivations other than profit maximization. But how far that has already happened is doubtful. Firstly, many of the 'new' motives which it is suggested now exist can be seen not as conflicting with profit maximization but as a shift in emphasis to *long-run* profit maximization. And, secondly, studies which have been made suggest that *owner* control persists to a remarkable degree. Michael Barratt Brown, for example, found that when he studied the top 120 companies 'about a third had boards consisting mainly of the owner and his family or nominees'.[8] In the United States, '*Fortune* reported that in 1966, controlling ownership of 150 of the 500 largest U.S. corporations rested in the hands of an individual or of the members of a single family.'[9]

Closer to the truth, then, is probably Marris's assertion that although capitalism today is 'overwhelmingly managerial there

8. M. Barratt Brown, *What Economics is About*, Weidenfeld & Nicolson, 1970, pp. 149–50.

9. Quoted in Bob Erith, *A Galbraithian Reappraisal: The Ideological Gadfly*, reprinted in E. K. Hunt and Jesse G. Schwartz, *A Critique of Economic Theory*, Penguin Modern Economics Readings, 1972.

nonetheless remains a sufficient number of traditional capitalists to be capable of significantly influencing the managers' behaviour.'

Profits and Efficiency. Profits, in the market model, perform the function of signalling switches of capital from one line of production to another – from inefficient to efficient uses. But in the real world of firms holding dominant market positions and being reluctant to engage in open price competition, they are in a position where they fix their own prices rather than accept them from the market. They are price-makers rather than price-takers and can continue to make high profits even when they are inefficient. In other words profits may indicate the degree to which they have established a monopoly position rather than how effectively they are using resources.

All in all, the traditional theory of the firm and the place it has in the market ideal is very remote indeed from reality. The nature of the firms themselves – the permanence of giant companies and the way in which their activities extend across both national and industrial frontiers – makes analysis of their operations infinitely more complex than can be handled by economists' tools. Their manipulation of demand, market-sharing and price-fixing all distort the simple ballot-box theory of the market. And their operations are based on private cost and benefit, ignoring the wider social costs and benefits which are external to them.

This divergence from the ideal means that scant reliance can be placed on market forces as they actually work in bringing about an acceptable use of resources. Moreover, the extent to which the economy is now dominated by industrial giants, often multi-national, raises profound questions of control and accountability which we shall be looking at later.

14

Principles of Income Distribution

The last two chapters have concentrated on consumers and producers and the relationship between them in the 'final goods market', where finished products and services are bought and sold. We have been looking at the divergence between the theory and practice of a market economy and questioning how far the theory is anyway an ideal.

But in addition to the final goods market there is also a set of 'factor markets' in which buyers and sellers of resources – land, labour and capital – are brought together. With what result? What determines the price of a factor of production like labour? What light does economics shed on the distribution of income between individuals and classes? In this chapter we shall concentrate on the question of the distribution of income from *work*. Why do doctors earn more than dustmen, managing directors more than miners? And can differentials as wide as those which we have be economically and morally justified?

The real world is one of enormously complex and often very extreme disparities in incomes. We will therefore approach it cautiously, first of all blandly assuming away all its complications and then re-introducing them one at a time.

Begin by imagining an economy in which three conditions hold good: (i) that perfect competition exists throughout; buyers and sellers of both final goods and factors of production like labour are all too small independently to influence the price of whatever it is that they are buying and selling; (ii) that labour is homogeneous – all workers are quite identical, both physically and mentally; (iii) that factors of production, including labour, are perfectly mobile between jobs and areas. Obviously these are all highly unrealistic assumptions. But if they did hold good, what prediction could we make about the distribution of income earned from work?

In such an extraordinary economy, incomes from work would be broadly equalized. Firms would hire workers to the point at which the extra wage they had to pay out was just covered by the extra revenue which they earned from the consequent increase in sales. In economists' jargon, wages would be equal to the marginal productivity of labour. But this would tend to be the same in all industries. Suppose that temporarily this were not so and that wages and marginal productivity in the car industry, for example, rose above those in coal-mining. The result would be that miners would leave the coalfields and move into the car-producing areas; the increased supply of labour would force down car workers' wages. Meanwhile the reduction in work-force would be pushing up wages in the mining industry. Free movement of homogeneous factors in a perfect market works to eliminate income differentials. And wages, like the price of anything else, are determined by demand and supply.

But not entirely. For, although we have assumed that workers are all identical, the jobs they do will still be very different. Some will be interesting, others dull; some in warm, congenial conditions, others dirty and dangerous. Therefore what will be equalized in this imaginary situation are not incomes, but *net advantages*. The net advantages of a job include not just what it pays but also its non-pecuniary aspects. What we might expect is that dustmen would receive rather higher wages than those in occupations which in themselves are more rewarding and satisfying – like, for example, university professors. The differential in earnings between the two jobs would depend on how much extra cash university professors needed to induce them to give up their comfortable chairs and take to the cold streets.

It is time to drop the absurd assumptions with which we started. For the major explanation of the wide disparities in income from work in the real world is that these conditions do *not* hold good. There is not perfect competition, labour is not homogeneous, and it is not perfectly mobile.

For a start, then, part of the wage differentials between groups of workers results from monopolistic bargaining by trade unions, able, through apprenticeship rules and other restrictions, to limit the supply of labour and keep its price artificially high. Differentials arise because workers are not all organized to the same extent and because bargaining power varies from industry to industry. However, although these 'imperfections' of the labour market certainly help to explain the difference in wage rates between, say, car workers in Oxford and textile workers in Blackburn, they are by no means the most important of the factors making for unequal distribution of income from work.

The second assumption to be dropped is that of homogeneity of labour. Workers differ from each other first of all because of an unequal dispersion of 'natural talent'. This term is used in the very broadest sense. To begin with, we come in very different shapes and sizes: some are physically strong, others dexterous, others again feeble or disabled. Beyond these, there are differences in other faculties. Some people are more intelligent, some have musical gifts which others lack, some have drive and verve, others are naturally slow or indolent. How far these qualities are inborn and how much they are due to environmental influences is a fascinating and important question which is beyond our present scope. The fact is, whether *we* like it or not, by the time a child begins school, marked differences in ability, temperament and motivation are already deeply rooted and more likely to be reinforced rather than reduced by formal education.

What are the economic implications? Some talents, like physical strength, are likely to be in abundant supply. Others, like the ability to play violin concertos, will be confined to a few. Those who possess a talent in short supply for which there is a positive demand will be able to earn what economists have termed a 'rent of ability'.

This concept – of economic rent – needs a little explanation. It has nothing directly to do with the rent which is paid for houses, but is defined as a payment to a factor in scarce supply over and above its transfer earnings. Take the case for example of a pop singer who before being discovered was working as a bricklayer. Let's also suppose that the only other job he could do, apart from singing, *is* bricklaying – at which he could make

£30 a week. Then this £30 is known as his transfer earnings – it is the amount which he could earn in his next-best occupation. Therefore, all that we have to pay him to continue to sing is marginally above £30. If in fact he earns tens of thousands a week, then all of that above £30 is economic rent. It is a payment to him over and above what is needed to keep him in his present occupation.

The reason why pop singers, film stars, footballers and the like often earn vast sums is twofold. Firstly, they have 'talents' which are in extremely scarce supply and cannot easily be increased. And, secondly, there is a demand for those talents. Just having a rare ability – to be able to wriggle one's ears, for example – does not guarantee high rent earnings. The amount of rent depends entirely on the *demand* for the scarce ability.

The concept of economic rent not only throws some light on exotic income disparities like these; it also helps to understand more mundane wage differentials. Suppose, for example, that private cars are banned from a city centre. This will mean that a great deal more public transport will have to be provided. More bus drivers will be needed and one way of attracting them will be to increase wages from, say, £30 a week to £35 a week. The £35 will have to be paid, of course, not just to the new recruits but also to the drivers who previously worked for the bus company. For *them*, the extra £5 is a rent element in their earnings. It is more than necessary to keep them bus-driving – because before they had been prepared to accept only £30 a week. In this case, however, the £5 is termed 'quasi-rent', being really only a short-term bonus arising from a temporary shortage of a particular skill which can be fairly easily increased in the long run.

As well as differences in 'natural ability' in the workforce, there are those which result from education and training. A great deal more time and money has been spent on preparing a doctor for his vocation than on a dustman. In terms of economic analysis, this can be seen as *investment* in human capital – investment in the sense that resources have been used in education and training which could otherwise have been currently consumed. The result is that there is no such thing as 'pure labour'. Nuclear physicists are highly 'capital-intensive', embodying a great deal of investment; others, like postmen, are much more 'labour-intensive' workers, with little training. And in economics, the return to capital is interest. Part of the differential between workers of different skills is therefore to be explained by the fact that earnings include an element of interest in addition to pure wages.

Finally, what is the effect of discarding the third assumption of our initial model – that labour is perfectly mobile? In the real world, free movement of workers is limited in a number of ways. Firstly, between areas: workers may be reluctant to move to more prosperous regions because of a host of uncertainties, expense and unwillingness to be uprooted. Secondly, between jobs of a similar kind within the same area: the level of skill required in coal-mining and engineering may be roughly the same, for example, but it may not be easy for the redundant coalminer to acquire the new engineering skills which would create an employment opportunity for him. Thirdly, and most restricted of all, is movement between different *classes* of job: social immobility. It may be possible for the doctor to become a dustman but the reverse is certainly quite out of the question. Of course, the dustman's *son* could become a doctor, but even his chances of doing so are generally much worse than those of the *doctor's* son. Certainly social mobility in Britain has increased considerably over recent decades, but it is still very limited. The continued existence of private education and the cumulative effects of initial income, wealth and environmental disparities combine to restrict entry into many professions to a tiny minority of the working population.

The effect of imperfect immobility is that there is not a single market for labour in the economy; instead it is fragmented into a large number of non-competing groups. *Within* each of these groups, earnings for similar sorts of work will be roughly brought into line by the forces of supply and demand and movement between jobs. Thus a rise in car workers' wages in Oxford will have some effect on the incomes of other semi-skilled labour in the area. What happens is that when the car industry is expanding and taking on more workers, shortages develop in the supply, for example, of painters and decorators, who, if the demand for their services remains unchanged, will be able to push up the prices which they charge to their customers. But *between* groups, on the other hand, economic forces will have little equalizing effect because of lack of movement between them. An increase in the salaries paid to university professors, for instance, will have no effect whatever on the wages paid to car workers.

It is at this point that we can begin to see the limitations of traditional economics in providing an adequate account of the differences in earnings from work. It does seem genuinely useful as providing an analytical framework within which differentials of various sorts can be categorized; we can see that disparities arise because of differential bargaining power, because of uneven dispersion of abilities and aptitudes, because of differences in education and training and because of highly imperfect mobility of labour. Earnings from work can be seen as an amalgam of pure wages, monopolistic surpluses, interest on investment in human capital and various elements of economic rent.

But what the theory does not really offer is an explanation of these differentials. Take, in particular, the gap between the earnings of non-competing groups. Traditional theory takes us only to the point of recognizing that one of the reasons for differentials between professional and manual workers is that there is practically no upward mobility between the two groups. But what decides the extent of the disparity between them? Why does one group earn, say, ten times as much as the other, rather than five times as much? On this question economics has little to say.

In fact such differentials are a reflection of our social valuations: they express what we think one group of workers *ought* to earn in comparison with others. Doctors get paid a great deal more than dustmen because, as a society, we 'value' their services more highly. Managing directors can command salaries fantastically in excess of earnings on the shop floor because, as a society, we have come to accept that this is right and proper. Film stars and the like earn the enormous sums they do because, as a society, we agree that scarce talents deserve high rewards.

These are the values which underly our present extremely

unequal distribution of income from work. They are seldom expressly articulated, but they are nonetheless an implicit element in the process of wage bargaining and salary determination.

It is time that they were made explicit. They *may* be valuations which the majority of people find perfectly defensible and acceptable. On the other hand, once they were exposed, the principles on which incomes are distributed might seem to many to be profoundly unfair. The important thing is that they should be brought into the open for discussion by everyone rather than just the economic cognoscenti. Such a debate has hardly yet begun despite the fact that the issues involved are basic to the solution of many of our present economic problems.

We have to examine both the economic necessity and the moral justifiability of inequality. Perhaps widely unequal incomes are a vital element in the efficient functioning of the economic system but are morally unjust. Perhaps they are both economically necessary *and* morally acceptable. And perhaps they are neither. It is to these real issues that we now turn.

Is Inequality Economically Necessary?

There are a number of grounds on which it can be argued that inequality is essential if the economy is to run as we want it to. The first of these concerns the relationship between income distribution, savings and economic growth.

The poor are not known for their thriftiness; indeed if they are very poor the whole of their income has to be used up in providing for their immediate needs. Generally speaking, the more an individual earns, the greater the amount he is able and willing to save. Some go further than this and suggest (although the evidence is by no means clear) that high-income groups save not only a larger absolute amount than low-income groups, but also a greater *proportion* of their income. Therefore the greater the inequality in the distribution of income, the larger the volume of savings which an economy is likely to generate. For society, these savings allow an accumulation of capital – stored-up production which has not been frittered away in current consumption. It enables more investment to take place in factories, machines and all the other factors needed for greater production in the future. More equality therefore means less saving, less economic growth. We can have more consumption today, but only at the price of less jam tomorrow.

Secondly, there is the matter of incentives. It is argued that, human nature being what it is, a hierarchical distribution of incomes makes people wish to better themselves – to rise up the income strata and emulate those above them whom they envy. Take away differentials and the incentive to work harder is lost. Once again, the effect will be a fall in output. Moreover, removal of differentials between jobs and regions will remove the inducement for workers to move from one job and area to another. The economy will become fossilized in a rigid pattern of production and lack the flexibility which is called for by rapidly changing technology. And how, in an egalitarian society, can people be persuaded to undertake those jobs which are dirty, dangerous or particularly demanding in other ways? Would, for example, young people be prepared to undertake the long hard sacrificial slog of high school, university and post-graduate training unless they knew that at the end of the road they would be rewarded for their efforts by being paid substantially more than those who opted out at an earlier stage?

One way of testing the strength of these arguments for inequality is to suppose that in this country, for example, a law was passed so that overnight incomes became broadly equalized. What would happen to the economy?

Taking the growth point first, whether the amount of personal savings would be reduced depends on a number of factors. Those whose incomes fell to the new average would save less. But those whose incomes rose would save more. Only if it is true that the rich save a greater *proportion* of their income than the poor would the fact that some now save less offset the greater saving which would be undertaken by others. Then again, many savings institutions which are now geared to the requirements of their richer clients would be forced to adapt to the new situation and devise schemes which would help to increase the propensity to save of the now average lower-income groups. Moreover, a further potential source of savings would be opened up by the elimination of the conspicuous consumption of the rich which the present highly unequal distribution of income and wealth makes possible. It was Keynes, after all, who said that during the nineteenth century 'capitalists were allowed the greater part of the national cake on condition that they didn't eat it', and it is doubtful whether that condition – that high personal incomes are heavily ploughed back into productive investment – holds good to anything like the same extent today. And, finally, the greater part of saving in a modern economy is not in fact done by individuals anyway; it is the province of firms and the State itself. If therefore the amount of personal saving in a more egalitarian economy turned out to be insufficient, the authorities could either encourage more institutional saving or do the job themselves through taxation. In any case, in previous chapters it was argued (a) that the volume of saving is only a contributory element in the growth process, and (b) that economic growth should not be an aim *per se*. On this argument, 'losses' under this heading (if indeed there were any as a result of equal income distribution) should perhaps not be taken too seriously.

And what of the argument that without income differentials there would be a major weakening of incentives to work, to move and to accept jobs which are particularly demanding? This is really very suspect. Would the managing director, since he was now being paid no more than any other worker, say, 'There's no longer any point in worrying myself with the power and responsibility of running this firm' – and go down and join them on the shop floor? Would school leavers really opt to go straight into industry at sixteen rather than suffer the rigours of further education once they realized that they were not going to command much higher incomes as a reward for their prolonged studies? Doubtless there would be cases like this. But not many, because in fact we do jobs, not just for the money involved, but because they happen to satisfy other personal urges (or, more sadly, because we lack the gifts to do the things that we would really like to do). Responsible posts would still be filled, because there are many people who *enjoy* taking decisions and holding positions of power. And even dirty and dangerous jobs would still be manned either by those who for some personal reason prefer them, or by those who are unable to find pleasanter or safer employment. An egalitarian world would not, unfortunately, automatically guarantee everyone the job opportunity of his first choice. But it would at least be one in which the reluctant dustman has the consolation of knowing that he is being paid as much as the professional man who has a more varied and comfortable position. And to a large extent, after all, one might expect the number of dirty and dangerous jobs to be reduced once incomes were more equally distributed. It is because many occupations have traditionally been low-paid that they have also become unpleasant; low pay has retarded mechanization which could remove some of the more disagreeable aspects of the work.

All in all, then, there are no clearly compelling economic reasons for income differentials, except perhaps to equalize the 'net advantages' of various jobs along the lines we discussed earlier. And this would be a distribution markedly different from the present one, in that the dustmen might well expect to receive a rather higher return than the doctor.

Is Inequality Morally Justifiable?

The moral case for inequality is even more tenuous. As we have seen, economics can be used to identify four sources of income disparities: variations in bargaining strength of working groups; uneven spread of abilities; differences in education and training; and imperfect mobility.

But those differentials which stem from the greater power of some groups over others – whether it is because they are better organized, or occupy a peculiarly strategic position in the economy, or are able effectively to determine their own incomes as managers do – are not obviously deserving of moral approbation. Then again, to be born clever or musical or physically strong is nothing but a matter of chance; it seems a somewhat odd morality which highly rewards those who have been lucky, while saying to the unintelligent, the tone-deaf and the physically disabled: 'Not only have you had the misfortune to be born with these handicaps. We will continue to penalize you for them for the rest of your life by employing you in uninteresting, unpleasant, ill-paid jobs.' (And the 'economic rent' payments to the talented are clearly not *necessary*, since by definition they are over and above what is required to keep people in their present occupations.)

Nor is the education/training justification for inequalities very convincing – the argument that those who have been prepared to make the sacrifice involved then deserve higher earnings analagous to interest payable on capital. Take the case of undergraduates, for example. In the first place, much of what they do at university should be classified as consumption rather than investment; they are there, not just because of their future prospects, but also because they enjoy being at college. Secondly, how far are they really making any 'sacrifice'? Certainly they have forfeited the earnings which they could have made between the age when they could have left school and the time when they become graduates. But these are likely to be minimal, given the fact that they would have lacked any significant qualifications. Moreover, during their time at university these losses are anyway partially offset by State grants and earnings from vacation jobs. And yet a university degree is still a passport to a lifetime of substantially higher incomes than the non-graduate is likely to earn.

To the extent that higher education *is* a genuine 'investment' and involves the use of resources (buildings, equipment and teachers) which could otherwise have been used for present consumption, who has made the necessary sacrifice? It is seldom the students themselves. Either it is their own parents who bear the cost, or it is the general taxpayer. If therefore it is right that interest should be paid on the capital tied up in higher education, it is parents and taxpayers who should receive it rather than the fortunate beneficiaries of extended education.

And, finally, what moral justification can there possibly be for the differentials (largely unexplained by economics) between the various non-competing groups in the economy? These disparities, as we have seen, come about chiefly because of the impediments in the way of movement between different classes of jobs. And such obstacles become cumulative in an economic system in which wealth can be handed down from generation to generation. It is here that those who advocate 'equality of opportunity' as the key to a fairer society miss the point that the principle of circular and cumulative causation will continue to operate so long as the starting point is one between initial unequals. Suppose, for example, that not only do we establish equal incomes throughout the economy but simultaneously abolish public schools and other manifestations of a socially divided system. All children will now be from homes with the same family income and attend exactly the same sort of schools. But who will benefit most? It will still tend to be the children of middle-class parents – from a home background in which learning is given priority, in which books and study facilities are made freely available. *Full* social equality means in the first place positive discrimination in favour of those who start with an initial handicap. Our own system, on the other hand, works on precisely the opposite lines, granting cumulative advantages to those who begin from a more favoured position.

To sum up, the practical outcome of the market with regard to income distribution is likely to be highly inegalitarian, with the gap between rich and poor tending to widen rather than diminish. Yet, on examination, there are no compelling economic reasons for income inequalities; and the social norms which lie behind market forces, when made explicit, embody an extremely dubious morality. If this is so, how can inequalities on the scale which exist in our own economy possibly be justified? How great they are and the fundamental problems which stem from them are the subjects of the following chapters.

15

Basic Inequalities

So much for the theory of distribution. Traditional economics provides a means of categorizing income differentials but does little to explain or justify them. And the case for inequality – in both practice and principle – turns out, on inspection, to be a very weak one. But just what are the facts of the matter? How much inequality is there in a modern industrial economy such as Britain? In this chapter we look at the various forms of inequality – in personal incomes, in the shares of national income going to different factors of production and in the distribution of national wealth.

First of all, then, the way in which incomes are distributed between individuals. Starting at the apex of the income pyramid, the top 1 per cent of income earners in this country command no less than 8 per cent of total pre-tax incomes (rather less, incidentally, than they manage to cream off in the United States or most underdeveloped countries). The top 10 per cent receive about 28 per cent of total incomes. And when we switch our attention to the other end of the scale, we find that the poorest 20 per cent of British families get only $7\frac{1}{2}$ per cent of the national income (and that, by the way, is a higher proportion than the 5 per cent which is the commonly quoted figure for the United States). Broadly, this is a distribution pattern found in most advanced capitalist countries – with some, such as Germany or France, rather more unequal, and others, such as Sweden or Israel, rather less so.

There is no more brilliantly vivid account of what those rather dry statistics mean in personal terms than that of Jan Pen,[1] who portrays a Grand Parade lasting just one hour during which the

1. J. Pen, *Income Distribution*, Allen Lane The Penguin Press, 1971.

whole of the British population march past in ascending order of
height, their heights corresponding to the levels of their incomes.
We, the spectators, are assumed to be of average height (that is,
we earn the average income for the economy as a whole). Pen
describes the dramatic unfolding of the spectacle as we see it
from our vantage point.

'We see tiny gnomes pass by, the size of a matchstick, a cigarette ... housewives who have worked for a short time and so have
got nothing like an anuual income, schoolboys with a paper
round ... It takes perhaps five minutes for them to pass.' The
next five or six minutes sees 'an increase by leaps and bounds. The
people still passing by are still very small ones – about three feet –
but they are noticeably taller than their predecessors ... They
include some young people ... very many old-age pensioners ...
divorced women ... owners of shops doing poor trade ... unemployed persons.' Next 'the ordinary workers about whom there is
nothing out of the ordinary except that they are in the lowest-
paid jobs. Dustmen, Underground ticket collectors, some miners.
The unskilled clerks march in front of the unskilled manual
workers ... We also see a large number of coloured persons ... It
takes almost fifteen minutes before the passing marchers reach a
height of substantially more than four feet. For you and me this is
a disturbing sight; fifteen minutes is a long time to keep seeing
small people pass who barely reach to our midriff.'

Nor, as this group finally passes, is there any immediate relief
from this macabre spectacle. Instead, 'we keep seeing dwarfs ...
After another ten minutes small people approach who reach to
our collar bones. We see skilled industrial workers, people with
considerable training. Office workers, respectable persons, so to
say. We know that the parade will last an hour and perhaps we
expected that after half-an-hour we would be able to look the
marchers straight in the eye, but that is not so. We are still looking down on the top of their heads, and even in the distance we
do not yet see any obvious improvement. The height is growing
with tantalizing slowness, and *forty-five minutes have gone by
before we see people of our own size arriving*' (italics added).

These are teachers, executive civil servants, clerical workers,
shopkeepers, insurance agents, foremen, a few farmers. But it is

the last six minutes of the parade which becomes sensational with the arrival of the top 10 per cent.

Modestly tall to begin with (about six feet six inches): headmasters, youngish university graduates, seamen, farmers, departmental heads. 'They are people who had never thought that they belonged to the top 10 per cent.'

And then the climax packed into the last few minutes. 'Giants suddenly loom up. A lawyer, not exceptionally successful: eighteen feet tall... The first doctors come into sight, seven or eight yards, the first accountants. There is still one minute to go, and now we see towering fellows. University professors, nine yards, senior officers of large concerns, ten yards, a Permanent Secretary thirteen yards tall, and an even taller High Court judge; a few accountants, eye surgeons and surgeons of twenty yards or more.'

'During the last seconds the scene is dominated by colossal figures people like tower blocks. Most of them prove to be businessmen, managers of large firms and holders of many directorships, and also film stars and a few members of the Royal Family ... Prince Philip, sixty yards ... Tom Jones: nearly a mile high ... John Paul Getty. His height is inconceivable: at least ten miles, and perhaps twice as much.'

What is disturbing about these figures, in view of the arguments of the previous chapter, is not just the concentration of income at the very top of the scale – the continued existence of the super-rich. It is the extent of the disparities which exist lower down the scale – between more ordinary mortals like the average worker and the average manager. And in this respect, Britain is perhaps somewhat exceptional amongst otherwise comparable economies. Why should it be necessary in this country that the ratio between their incomes should be 1:10, whereas in Japan, for example, it is only 1:4?

It can be argued that the picture of massive inequalities which has emerged so far is exaggerated because the incomes which we have been comparing are *pre*-tax. With a taxation system which is progressive – taking a greater *proportion* of richer people's incomes – inequality should appear much less if we compare *post-tax* incomes. However, studies which have been made into this elusive subject do not offer clear evidence that this is so. Partly this is because the British tax system is anyway only partly progressive; in addition to income taxes, there are indirect taxes falling on rich and poor consumers alike simply according to what they buy – and indirect taxes have been increasing rather than diminishing as a proportion of total government revenue. Secondly, higher-income groups tend on the whole to find the process of tax avoidance a great deal easier than those lower down the income scale; the professional financial and accounting journals are full of advertisements offering a whole range of methods for reducing tax burdens. And, thirdly, there is the problem of defining precisely what should be included in the concept of income itself; higher income groups tend to enjoy not only larger monetary rewards, but also a much greater range of fringe benefits. Consequently, it is not altogether surprising to find in a study [2] made in 1959 that the bottom 25 per cent of income recipients paid 29·9 per cent of their income in taxes of one kind or another, while the top 5 per cent income-earners contributed a similar 28 per cent. In other words, the overall impact of the tax system has been proportional rather than progressive.

But if income is still very unequally distributed, has there not been a considerable narrowing of inequality over the years? Research suggests that this is so, and that redistribution was particularly marked in the period between 1938 and 1955. Lydall's calculations, for example, suggest that the share of income going to the top 1 per cent was dramatically halved from 16·2 per cent in 1938 to 8 per cent in 1955, and that the share of the top 5 per cent fell over the same period from 12·8 per cent to 10·2 per cent.[3] It seems clear that a major redistribution did take place, although its extent may be exaggerated by the fact that the top group increasingly took their incomes in forms which the figures conceal.[4]

However, the evidence is that this was a once-and-for-all reslicing of the national cake. The process of redistribution towards lower-income groups has not continued. On the contrary, during

2. H. F. Lydall, *Journal of the Royal Statistical Society*, 1959.
3. ibid.
4. R. M. Titmuss, *Income Distribution and Social Change*, Allen & Unwin, 1962.

the late sixties and early seventies, there are pointers that the poor may have become relatively poorer. This is partly because the middle-income groups tend to use social services – for example, higher education – much more extensively than those in the lower-income strata; partly because they are able to capitalize on tax concessions to a greater extent (a classic example is the extent to which those fortunate enough to own their houses have their mortgage interest subsidized); and partly because over those years there was a substantial increase in a number of regressive taxes – increases in local authority rents and rates, in national insurance and health contributions – coupled with withdrawals of subsidies on, for instance, food and school milk.

The mass of people in this country have never been better off than they are today, as can be judged by the extent to which the average family owns consumer durables like cars, radio and television and washing machines. Affluence today is more dispersed than ever before – and indeed an economic system based on mass standardized production demands that this should be so. But this is not to say that inequality is consequently decreasing. The poor are as a whole not getting absolutely poorer, although some may be. But there has been a tendency in recent years for their *relative* poverty to increase.

So far we have been concentrating on the unequal distribution of income. But inequality takes on a new dimension when we look at the way in which *wealth* is distributed. Extreme disparities in income are dwarfed by those in the ownership of personal wealth, which are, as a distinguished Cambridge economist has put it, 'really fantastic'. [5] And Professor Meade is not one who is prone to hyperbole or the expression of revolutionary sentiments.

By personal wealth is meant holdings of physical assets like houses, land and consumer durable goods, and financial assets such as bank and building society deposits, stocks and shares. Dividing the total personal wealth in Britain in the early seventies amongst the adult population as a whole would give an average holding for each married couple of about £8,000. The

5. J. E. Meade, *Efficiency, Equality and the Ownership of Capital*, Allen & Unwin, 1964.

most recent study [6] of the distribution of wealth in Britain produces some startling results. Professor Atkinson suggests that the top 1 per cent wealth-holders in fact own 29 per cent of the total personal wealth in the country. The top 5 per cent hold over half the total. The remainder is shared by the other 95 per cent of the population, and even within this range the distribution is extremely unequal.

Moreover, inequality has a qualitative as well as a quantitative aspect. Those with greater wealth are able to hold it in far more *profitable* forms than those at the lower end of the scale, in particular, in stocks and shares and investment properties with high yields and capital gains potential. Thus by the mid-sixties, for example, only 4 per cent of the adult population owned any shares at all, and 1 per cent owned four-fifths of the total of privately held shares. The result is that the top 10 per cent wealth-holders earned no less than 99 per cent of total personal income from property-holding of one kind or another.

At the very top, Professor Atkinson estimates there are probably in Britain today ninety-two people who are worth more than £2½ million. In other words, these individuals own over one thousand times the wealth of the average man. This can be compared with the top ninety-two managing directors who, with income averaging about £60,000, earn some forty times as much as the average worker. As Atkinson comments, 'The difference between the top wealth-holders and the average person (let alone those whose wealth is below the average) is much greater than in the case of earnings. The magnitude of the gap is quite staggering.'

The concentration of wealth in very few hands has certainly been reduced over the years: it has been estimated that in the first decade of the century the top 1 per cent owned 65–70 per cent of total personal wealth. But the evidence also suggests that the trend to increased equality has subsequently been halted, in spite of apparently penal rates of death duties imposed on large estates. What has happened, as with incomes, is that methods of avoidance have become increasingly sophisticated, with the result that further redistribution has largely taken place *within*

6. A. B. Atkinson, *Unequal Shares*, Allen Lane The Penguin Press, 1972.

the top strata of wealth-holders through gifts and trust schemes in anticipation of death-duty commitments. Payment of death-duty has become a largely optional matter, undertaken only by the foolish and ignorant or those with a peculiarly heightened social conscience.

How have these massive inequalities come about? Suppose that we begin with a primitive market economy made up of individuals none of whom possess any wealth and all of whom have equal incomes. How will it develop? [7] At *Stage I*, income differentials will soon emerge – if only because of the uneven dispersion of talents. Similarly, inequality in wealth will also appear, partly because the richer can afford to save more, but also simply as a result of the age distribution of the population – with the old having had more time to accumulate capital than the young. *Stage II* is an interesting one, where a combination of social and genetic factors come into play. Birds of a feather mix together. There will be a tendency for marriages to take place between those of similar 'intelligence' or talents, and between those whose income levels brings them into closest contact. Genetically, the implication seems to be that although, on average, the children of highly intelligent parents will be of lower intelligence than themselves, there is also a greater chance of their offspring being exceptionally intelligent. Thus there are both levelling-up and levelling-down elements at work – but also a polarization of the extremes. To the extent that intelligence and talents are associated with earning power, the overall effect will be disequalizing. *Stage III* introduces the association of earning power with property ownership. Those with higher incomes will not only be able to save more, but, as we have seen, save in more profitable ways. *Stage IV* depends on the inheritance system: primogeniture enables a further consolidation of wealth, disequalizing to the extent that the subsequent generations are capable of at least retaining their inherited fortunes. By *Stage V*, the full cumulative forces begin to work. Initial natural advantages leading to accumulated wealth, passed on in the form of inherited riches, generate further acquired advantages of wealth. The rich can buy superior education for their children

7. What follows is a stylization of the analysis in Meade, op. cit.

and set them up in businesses and professions in which the personal contacts between groups of like-minded people are vital. And the 'poor' are further impoverished because the quality of non-private education, for example, is kept low because those very parents most likely to agitate for its improvements, the rich and vocal, are those who have opted out. Finally, by *Stage VI*, there develops an association between earning power, wealth and *ruling* power. The rich become strong enough to inculcate their own élitist ethos into a society and to achieve effective control over the legislature, the administration and mass media in a way best serving their own ends. All of this happens without any conscious conspiracy on the part of the rich. The argument is simply that, once an initial inequality is established, market forces work to widen rather than diminish the gap between the rich and the poor, the privileged and the underprivileged.

Thus inequalities of income and wealth are mutually reinforcing. In the last chapter we dealt only with disparities in income earned from *work*. But however great the differential between the average worker and the average managing director, it is nothing compared with the income gap between 'earned' and 'unearned' income resulting from ownership or wealth.

But would policies aimed at redistributing wealth be anything more than an emotional gesture? While it is admitted that wealth is concentrated in the hands of a very few, it is often said that to spread it out over the population as a whole would be a mere drop in the ocean. In fact, as Atkinson points out, this is simply not true. If wealth in Britain *were* to be equally distributed amongst the adult population, the resulting *income* from it would amount to no less than an average of nine pounds a week for each married couple.[8]

There is a third aspect of distribution apart from that of income and wealth between individuals. That is the way in which national income is shared out functionally between the various factors of production. In particular, what are the proportions going to wages and profits? This is a matter about which there has been a continuing controversy for many years. Supporters

8. Atkinson, op. cit.

of capitalism try to prove that the share of labour in national income has progressively increased over the years. Marxist critics, on the other hand, anxious to show that capitalism has meant growing exploitation of labour, have usually argued that the share of wages has tended to decline.

The facts of the matter are very difficult to establish. Evidence can be found for variants of either case, depending on how the various elements are defined. What, for example, is meant by 'labour'? Does it include managing directors and employees in government service? Or should it be confined to manual workers in the private sector in order to highlight what would happen under unregulated capitalism? How should the self-employed be treated, since their income is generally a combination of both wages and profits? Should the basic division of national income be simply twofold – between income from work and other income? Or should 'other income' be broken down into interest, rent and profit?

Depending on how these questions are answered – and none is more 'correct' than another – very different interpretations can be put on the present distribution and the way in which it has changed historically. Table 9 shows a division between three groups: wages and salaries (that is, with 'labour' being treated in the broadest sense), rents, and a third category of profits, interest and mixed incomes (avoiding the difficulties of sorting out the different functional elements in the earnings of the self-employed). On this basis, it can be seen that, over the past century, the share of 'labour' has dramatically increased at the expense of other forms of income.

Table 9: Percentage shares of national income

	Wages/salaries	Rents	Profits/interest/other income
1860–69	48·5	13·7	38·9
1900–1909	48·4	11·4	40·2
1920–29	59·7	6·6	33·7
1940–49	68·8	4·9	26·3
1960–65	74·0	6·0	20·0

However, to a large degree these figures simply reflect the conversion over the period of small businesses into public companies, with the result that former proprietors earning 'mixed incomes' become part of the salariat. But there has also been an upgrading of labour as more and more investment has come to be embodied in it. Greater education means that the labour force today is of a very different quality from that of a century ago; to that extent, there has been a redistribution of income from physical capital in favour of human capital. The increased share of labour defined in the broad sense has been at the expense of interest (as the quantity of capital has increased) and rent (as the relative importance of agriculture has declined). What seem to have remained remarkably constant, on the other hand, are the shares of manual workers – at about 40 per cent of national income – and profits.

Constancy of profits has been questioned in a recent Marxist study,[9] which suggests that during the sixties an increase in worker militancy substantially eroded the profit share of national income. This breakthrough heralded either the demise of capitalism or efforts by the capitalist establishments to restore profitability at the expense of the working class. But neither the delight of the extreme left that Marxist predictions were at last coming true or the gloomy foreboding of the leader-writers in the financial press seem justified on the evidence to date. Profits *always* decline during the downturn of a cycle and in the particularly severe recession of the late sixties might have been expected to fall more than usual. But in the upturn of 1972 and 1973 they rose rapidly, and it is at least premature to assert that there is any clear trend towards a reduced profit ratio.

What should we conclude from this about the effectiveness of trade unions? Despite the fact that their demands are frequently couched in the language of confrontation, they have not succeeded in a century and a half of struggle to bring about any major redistribution at the expense of profits. Partly this is because of the ability of firms to pass increased wage costs on to the consumer through higher prices. And partly it is due to the competitive sectionalism of trade unions, which means that much of their effort is dissipated in bargaining about differentials

9. A. Glyn and R. Sutcliffe, *British Capitalism, Workers and the Profits Squeeze*, Penguin Books, 1972.

between themselves with a consequent 'phoniness about the inter-necine struggle between unions, and between their official and unofficial leaders. The struggles are real enough, but they hardly relate to the extreme inequalities within the society.'[10]

Not that it is obvious that profits are the appropriate target in any case. There is nothing inherently evil about profit. Indeed, surpluses earned by enterprises can serve two useful economic functions – as indicators of relative efficiency and in generating funds for investment in new capacity. But in practice, as we have seen, profits may reflect not efficiency but the fact that a firm has achieved a dominant market position which it can duly exploit. The efficiency which profits measure is calculated on the basis of private costs and revenues and ignores social gains and losses. And profit – directly when it is distributed as dividends, indirectly when it is ploughed back – benefits only that tiny proportion of the total population in whose hands personal wealth is largely concentrated.

10. I. Bowen, *Acceptable Inequalities*, Allen & Unwin, 1970, p. 127.

16

The Quest for Equity

Incomes policy is a notion which some people see as so imbued with an irradicable immorality that they cannot bring themselves to discuss the matter at all. For others, it represents a quite unnecessary and irrelevant obstruction of the workings of the market. For others again – and our experience is that nearly every government sooner or later comes round to this point of view – it represents the only hope of coming to grips with the problem of inflation in modern industrial economies.

With the first of these groups of opinion, those who reject incomes policy out of hand as socially quite unacceptable, we can easily agree that as they have been practised to date they have always been basically unfair; but that should not preclude a search for a set of policies which *would* be just and command general acceptance. To those who retain a faith in uncurbed market forces we have already provided an answer: that in practice the outcome of the market for income and wealth distribution is even more profoundly inequitable and irrational, representing as it does the results of imperfections, the dominance of large firms and unions, and barriers to mobility. The third group, on the other hand, who recognize that inflation will be brought under control only through incomes policies, are almost certainly right. But they are wrong if they think that it is simply a matter of tinkering with a system of income determination which otherwise remains basically unchanged – if incomes policy is seen merely as a technical device for coping with the specific problem of rising prices.

In this chapter we shall not be concerned with the minutiae of incomes policy – its past failures, present shortcomings or future modifications. It is more important first to get agreement about what its underlying principles ought to be. And the policy for incomes which will be discussed here is not narrowly aimed at containing prices but instead faces up to the central issue of inequality of which inflation is only one of a number of undesirable by-products.

The question, then, is one of economic justice. There is undoubtedly a growing dissatisfaction, more particularly amongst the young, with an economic system which generates blatant inequities. The conventional indicators of economic success – measured by growth rates, the balance of payments surplus or even the level of employment – seem to many people irrelevant compared to the question of fairness. They are less concerned about what is happening to the economy as a whole than how it affects *them*, where they stand in relation to others, whether or not they are being done down and what they can do about it.

This quest for greater equity is a natural product of a number of forces which have developed over the years to give people a greater awareness of the total situation and their position in it. 'Universal education has taken away from the minority the power of exclusive knowledge.'[1] In this process the mass media have played an important part. The downstairs are no longer ignorant of the goings-on upstairs. We are all intimately acquainted with the life-styles of those in different social circumstances from our own. Moreover there has been a marked increase in the power of organized labour, and modern industry is so complex and interdependent that it is not merely mass unions who are able to strike a hard bargain; quite small groups of workers can be equally powerful if they are engaged in strategically important occupations on which much larger industries depend.

These momentous changes inevitably subject society to enormous social and economic stresses which can be summed up in the frank admission of a 'young Conservative lawyer' that 'It's all right when only 5 per cent of the population are grabbing, the trouble is when the other 95 per cent start playing the game.'[2]

1. R. Maudling, *The Times*, 12 September 1972.
2. Quoted in G. Turner, *Towards a New Philosophy for Industrial Society*.

In this game, inflation plays a stabilizing role in providing a safety-valve through which a variety of social and economic tensions can be released. It creates an arena in which battles can be fought without real bullets. It is a game in which nearly everyone, or everyone with bargaining strength or vocal enough to be electorally significant, can at some stage or other claim to be on the winning side. Admittedly, the gains may be only ephemeral or even illusory. To a large extent Keynes was right when he argued that

a demand on the part of the Trade Unions for an increase in money rates of wages to compensate for every increase in the cost of living is futile, and greatly to the disadvantage of the working class. Like the dog in the fable, they lose the substance in gaping at the shadow. It is true that the better organized sections might benefit at the expense of other consumers. But except as an effort at group selfishness, as a means of hustling someone else out of the queue, it is a mug's game to play. In their minds and hearts the leaders of the Trade Unions know this as well as anyone else. They do not want what they ask. But they dare not abate their demands until they know what alternative policy is offered.[3]

That alternative can only be one which openly examines the way in which incomes are now determined and questions the distribution of income and wealth which results from it. Widespread dissatisfaction with the present outcome is shown by the results of a recent study[4] which suggest that only 19 per cent of the population think that the current share-out of wages among different jobs in Britain is at all fair. And this study deals only with the distribution of wage income. It can hardly be doubted that, if the same question was asked about share-out between wage and management incomes and between incomes from work and wealth, and about the distribution of wealth itself, an even greater proportion would argue that the present situation is iniquitous.

We have already looked at the facts of the matter and argued that the economic case put forward by supporters of inequality –

3. J. M. Keynes, *How to Pay for the War*, Macmillan, 1940.
4. *Report on the Study of Some Aspects of National Job Evaluation*, North Paul and Associates Ltd, 1973.

that, for example, it provides incentives and a source of capital accumulation without which the economy would function very ineffectively – is far from convincing. Nor is there any clear moral justification for major disparities. And yet the burden of proof surely lies with these opponents of equality. As Sir Isaiah Berlin has put it: 'If I have a cake and there are ten persons among whom I wish to divide it, then if I give exactly one tenth to each, this will not, at any rate automatically, call for justification; whereas if I depart from this principle of equal division I am expected to produce a special reason.'[5]

Presumption and morality both point towards egalitarianism. And so, for that matter, does traditional economic theory – although, in providing an analytical framework in which inequalities can be understood, it has frequently been taken as implicitly justifying them. In fact, however, classical economic thinking is logically egalitarian in its implications. Thus in the theory of consumer behaviour there is a concept of 'diminishing marginal utility', which simply means that the more you have of something the less you desire a bit more of it. It is a concept which can be applied not only to bread or television sets or ballpoint pens, but also to money itself (except in the case of misers). The result is that to give a pound to a very rich man will afford him far less satisfaction than giving it to a very poor man. Similarly, taking away a pound from the rich and redistributing it to the poor will be likely to increase total satisfaction (provided that they have the same capacity for enjoyment). It was on this basis that Sir Dennis Robertson, one of the more 'reactionary' and brilliant economists of the orthodox school, used to have to argue for equality in terms of 'passionate reluctance'.

But what does equality of income distribution mean? Should every person receive exactly equal pay, regardless of age, effort and the sort of job he or she does or does not do? Or does equality mean similar pay for similar work? Or should needs be taken into account – for example, the different family responsibilities of otherwise identical workers? These are interesting questions which, however, we can for the time being safely

5. Quoted in A. B. Atkinson, *Unequal Shares*, p. 79.

ignore. That is because they fall into the same class as sociologists' claims that a society requires a hierarchical ordering, and the fears expressed by, for example, Sir Roy Harrod, that 'high civilization and culture' might be adversely affected by too much equality. These are all bridges which can be crossed if ever we come to them. It is premature to worry about such niceties in a world of massive inequalities which, at times, are actually being widened rather than narrowed. 'In practice,' as one seeker of minimum acceptable inequality has put it, 'the danger seems more often that the public authorities will fail to go far enough, not that they may go too far.'[6] When we have reduced income differentials from their present extremes to, for example, 5 : 1, that will be the time when the question how much further the pursuit of equality should go will become relevant.

Wage–Wage Inequalities

The problems involved in reducing inequality arise at a number of different levels, some more intractable than others. We begin with what ought to be the easiest aspect of the question – the principles on which incomes should be distributed between wage-earners. Suppose that we take present differentials as a starting point and ask on what basis future wage increases should be awarded. There are a number of possibilities.

One would be to confine wage increases to cases of proven productivity improvements. But in practice labour productivity is only partly a matter of workers making greater efforts. More usually it results from the introduction of more efficient techniques. All in all, it is a matter of chance whether a worker is in an industry which has worked inefficiently in the past (thus giving considerable scope for improvement now) or in one particularly susceptible to technological innovation – or whether he has the bad luck to be employed in an industry with a good past record or where new techniques are difficult to apply. There seems no reason at all why the fruits of increased national productivity should be distributed in this way, and certainly the effect is likely to be further disequalizing.

6. I. Bowen, *Acceptable Inequalities*, p. 48.

There is perhaps even less to be said for giving everyone the same percentage increase. Existing differentials would be permanently frozen; and the lowest-paid workers would suffer worst, since their absolute increases would be less than those on a higher initial starting-point.

The only obvious ways of reducing wage differentials are either to concentrate any hand-out at the lower end of the scale, or to give all wage-earners the same flat-rate increase. The first of these would represent a direct attack on wage inequalities; the second would reduce *relative* differentials between different groups although the absolute gap between them would always remain the same. However, a proposal along the latter lines in the course of discussions between the government and the T.U.C. in 1972 failed to secure acceptance. It is important to see why.

Partly, it was due to factors which will be discussed in a later section – the fact that incomes policy was seen as essentially an exercise in *wage restraint*. Why, in those circumstances, should groups of workers in particularly strong positions be denied their share of the spoils of the jungle? Why should *they* be singled out as responsible for the less fortunate members of the working class? But beyond this there is the sectionalist nature of British trade unions, which means that they often have a vested interest *against* narrowing of inequalities. Their job is not to serve the working class as a whole but to look after their own members. Very often this implies maintaining or widening differentials rather than reducing them.

The resulting wage relativities were described by the National Board for Prices and Incomes as frequently 'inequitable, irrational and arbitrary'. One possible approach to the problem is to apply more widely the techniques of job evaluation. This involves a description of what is involved in various jobs, a comparison between them and a ranking of different kinds of work according to what are considered relative criteria.

Extended use of job evaluation could serve a number of useful functions. In the first place, it would help to identify 'like with like' situations, where almost exactly the same job is being performed by workers of similar training and skills earning quite different wages. Job evaluation would help to clear up anomalies like this by indicating that the two ought to be brought into line. And, secondly, if negotiators had to justify differential wage claims within terms of job evaluation, a much-needed element of rationality would be introduced into bargaining.

However, the virtue of job evaluation is certainly not that it is objective. At first sight it might appear to offer a scientific way of ranking jobs and determining differentials free from the partiality and prejudice of the present system of wage-fixing. It does nothing of the sort. It is one thing to agree, for example, that the work of a building labourer and a local authority road-maintenance worker are closely comparable. But how do we set about comparing the building labourer with a nurse or bus driver? The building labourer needs little training but a good deal of physical strength; he has an outside job often in unpleasant conditions; job security may be low and he will find the work harder going as he gets older. The nurse has had a lengthy training, must be willing to perform unpleasant tasks, be patient and humane, and accept considerable responsibility. But does the nurse have more or less responsibility than the bus driver, who, apart from concern about the safety of his passengers, must have the appropriate reflexes, judgement and temperament?

Ranking quite different occupations such as these involves first of all setting out what we think are relevant criteria – for example, length of training, responsibility, physical strength and degree of unpleasantness; we then have to attach *weights* to each of them. Should responsibility count more than physical strength – and, if so, by how much? Clearly this is anything but an objective procedure. It depends on our point of view. It involves making social value judgements. However, this is a strength of job evaluation rather than a weakness. It is a technique which forces us to make explicit values which are concealed in the present horse-dealing method of wage determination. That, too, implies values – and once they are brought out into the open for public discussion, it may well be that most people find them quite unacceptable.

In this respect, the results of a recent study already referred to are extremely interesting.[7] Two panels were formed, one comprising 'experts' from management and trade unions and the other made up of 'laymen' like wage-earners and housewives. They were then asked to compare and rank twenty-three sample jobs. The results are shown below.

	Expert panel	*Lay panel*
Group 1	Miner	Miner
	Male nurse	Male nurse
	Maintenance craftsman	
Group 2		
	Ambulance driver	Maintenance craftsman
	Compositor	Ambulance driver
	Able seaman	Compositor
	Farm worker	Able seaman
	Heavy-goods vehicle driver	Farm worker
	Bricklayer	Heavy-goods vehicle driver
	Gasboard fitter	Bricklayer
		Railway guard
Group 3	Railway guard	Gasboard fitter
	Weaver	Weaver
	Docker	Docker
	Chemical process worker	Chemical process worker
		Car production worker
Group 4	Car production worker	
	Postman	Postman
	Industrial storekeeper	Industrial storekeeper
	Press operator	Press operator
	Refuse collector	Refuse collector
	Bus conductor	Bus conductor
	Fork-lift truck operator	Fork-lift truck operator
	Shop assistant	Shop assistant
Group 5	Factory cleaner	Factory cleaner

Another part of the experiment was to check the results of the two panels against the view of the general public by means

7. *Report on the Study of Some Aspects of National Job Evaluation*, op. cit.

of a national questionnaire in which respondents were asked to rank a list of twelve manual occupations. This was the outcome:

1. Underground miner
2. Ambulance driver
3. Maintenance craftsman
4. Heavy-goods vehicle driver
5. Farm worker
6. Bricklayer
7. Docker
8. Car production worker
9. Refuse collector
10. Railway guard
11. Bus conductor
12. Factory cleaner

There are obviously two very interesting aspects of this exercise. Firstly, there is the extent to which the two panels and respondents to the questionnaire were in agreement. There are remarkably few deviations in their ranking order, and those are only minor ones. And, secondly, the way in which the participants thought that the jobs *ought* to be ordered is very different from the hierarchy of pay scales which actually exist. Very low-paid groups like ambulance drivers and farm workers come high in the job evaluation list, while highly paid workers in the car industry are ranked well below them.

So far we have been concerned only with differentials within the wage sector. We now turn to a much more important set of disparities – those between wage earners and other recipients of income from work.

Wages and Other Incomes from Work

The incomes of those in management or the professions differ from wage-earners' in two main respects. Firstly, they are often much more amorphous in character. The coal-miner may get his free coal, the office girl her lunch vouchers. But these are clearly of a quite different degree from supplementary forms of 'income' which the upper echelons receive in addition to their basic salaries and fees: pension rights, golden handshakes, subsidized housing, the company car and expense account. And, secondly, at least in the private sector, the incomes of top management, lawyers, accountants and the like are largely self-determined rather than the result of any collective bargaining process.

The result, as we have seen, is extreme inequality in income distribution. Applying the technique of job evaluation again, it is obvious that disparities such as these could only be justified if extremely high weightings were given to qualities like length of academic and professional training, ability to take decisions, exercise authority and assume responsibility. However, the argument of a previous chapter was that such weightings are both economically unnecessary and morally dubious. Moreover, a sizable proportion of top-income earners' emoluments arise from the fact that they work in occupations from which the majority are excluded by social immobility. In other words, part of their income is 'economic rent' – by definition, in excess of what they need to be paid.

It is just possible that there exists a national consensus that present income inequalities from work are totally justified. We do not know because there has so far been no open and systematic debate on the subject. But until there is we are in the highly unsatisfactory position that, as Pen puts it, 'salaries emerge which reflect *somebody's* social preferences. These are . . . the preferences of the decision-makers – social groups whose size and locations are not known, but which in any case form a selection from the population. Norms are used that are not explicit and not open to discussion.' [8]

There are three broad lines along which inequalities such as these can be reduced. The first is one which can only be effective in the very long run, and that is to attack the causes of social immobility which are a major cause of disparities. This can only be achieved by fundamental reform of the educational system substantially to widen access to a range of occupations now confined to a privileged few. In practical terms this must mean the abolition of a private fee-paying system of education run in

8. J. Pen, *Income Distribution*, p. 324.

parallel with that provided by the State. Whether by educating their children privately parents actually buy them a higher quality of education or merely a passport into restricted social circles, there can be no doubt that the continued existence of public schools are a central element in the process of self-perpetuating inequalities. In fact, egalitarianism requires much more than equality of educational opportunity. What is needed is positive discrimination in favour of initially less-privileged groups – quite the opposite of the situation as it is, where children born in industrial slums or coloured ghettoes are likely to find themselves still further under-privileged by attending overcrowded and antiquated schools unable to attract good teaching staff easily.

A second approach is to treat the symptoms. If the gap between incomes from work are thought to be intolerably wide, it is open to the State to siphon off excessive earnings through more progressive taxation. There are certainly difficulties, because, as a general rule, the higher the income, the greater the possibilities for tax evasion and tax avoidance. And, once again, in practice we are moving in the opposite direction. Thus, for example, the tax changes operative in 1973–4 announced in the 1972 Budget amounted to a substantial redistribution to high-income groups. At a time when the government was urging acceptance of an incomes policy limiting pay rises to 4 per cent plus £1, income tax changes then beginning to take effect were increasing the take-home pay of those earning £10,000 by 5.5 per cent, those on £20,000 by 15 per cent, the £30,000 group by 28 per cent, and the lucky £50,000 income-earners by a staggering 49 per cent.[9]

The third approach is a more direct one. *If* we are aiming at greater equality, then it is more logical to reduce pre-tax disparities rather than try to soak them away through taxation. But how can this be done in a situation in which, as we have already pointed out, top-income groups largely determine their own rates of pay? This can only come about if the government itself accepts full responsibility for determining differentials *or* if a public consensus emerges which puts social pressure on high-

9. Trade Union Research Unit.

income groups to accept lower remuneration *or* if the power structure is changed so that workers in an industry are involved in the process of determining not only their own wage rates but those above and below them. We shall have more to say on this last possibility in a later chapter.

The examples of Sweden and Israel suggest that there would be powerful resistance from professional groups threatened by policies aimed at achieving substantially greater equality. In Britain, on the other hand, even the principles involved are not in the forefront of public debate, let alone the practical difficulties in reducing inequality. We have been content to pay lip-service to greater equality as a vague ideal and pretend that our taxation system is gradually bringing it about.

Income from Work and Income from Wealth

Earlier chapters have already stressed the contribution of massive concentrations of personal wealth to widening inequalities in income distribution. The incomes of the very richest members of society result mostly not from work, but from their holdings of assets. The extent to which an uneven distribution of personal wealth has a skewing effect on income distribution is reinforced by two further considerations. Firstly, the greater an individual's wealth-holding, the more profitable are the sort of assets in which he can invest. And, secondly, although taxation of unearned income is at steeply progressive rates, the element of capital gains is taxed relatively lightly. Since the rich have the benefit of abundant professional advice, it is not difficult for them to enjoy the fruits of their wealth in the form which attracts the least tax burden.

Unequal incomes from work lead to inequalities of wealth holding, which, coupled with the process of inheritance, perpetuate still wider disparities in incomes. In Britain, this continues to be the case, despite apparently penal rates of estate duty which might have been expected, over the course of the present century, to have very substantially equalized the distribution of personal wealth. Looking at the top 1 per cent of the population this certainly seems to have happened: their share fell from 69 per cent in 1911–13 to about 40 per cent in 1960.[10] However, this has been accompanied by a substantial *increase* in the share of the next 4 per cent. Suspicion that the effect of estate duty has therefore been chiefly to re-shuffle wealth amongst the richest themselves is supported by the ease and variety of methods by which payment of estate duty can be avoided. These methods, it should be stressed, are perfectly legal. It is simply a matter of taking advantage of loopholes in the law which are widely advertised and yet about which governments have been disinclined to take any significant action. Indeed, payment of high estate duty has become almost optional. 'Whenever a particularly large estate is reported in the press with the duty paid representing between 60 per cent and 80 per cent of the value of the estate, the deceased is regarded as an eccentric.'[11]

It is not that we do not *know* how to reduce inequalities in wealth. A great deal of work has already been done devising ways in which greater equality could be achieved. What is lacking is the political will to take effective action. It is difficult to avoid the conclusion that measures to reduce the inequality of wealth in this country, like schemes for land reform in many under-developed nations, are put on the statute book with the tacit understanding that they will not be rigorously applied.

'Incomes policies', as they have been practised by successive post-war governments, have failed. They have failed because they have always been introduced in response to an immediate and urgent *crisis*. They have failed because they have been solely directed towards the solution of the problem of inflation. They have failed because of their transience – no one has ever expected them to survive as a permanent machinery. They have failed, above all, because they have always been regarded by large sections of the population as profoundly *unfair*.

And yet fairness is what incomes policies should be about. That should be their principal aim – the achievement of greater equity. Only when a new social consensus emerges concerning

10. Atkinson, op. cit., p. 22.

11. J. R. S. Revell, *The Wealth of the Nation*, quoted in Atkinson, op. cit., p. 125.

the old-fashioned but crucial question of equality will incomes policies become viable and assume their proper role as a permanent mechanism for bringing about a greater measure of economic justice. And only then, incidentally, will inflation become controllable.

17

What Pattern of Output?

Economists and governments have spent a great deal of time and effort in the post-war years in trying to find ways in which more output can be produced from our limited resources. But the fact that the productive capacity of the economy *has* increased over this period, albeit sporadically, is not due to any major theoretical or policy breakthrough. We are still largely ignorant about the precise causes and processes of economic growth and how to influence them.

However, as was argued in Chapter 10, economic growth is not anyway an end in itself. It is quite irrational to set up increased output as a policy goal without reference to what the increased output is made up of. And yet this is what we have done. We have gone for quantity regardless of quality. Seeking answers to the question of how to achieve *more* production, we have too often forgotten to ask – production *of what*? It is this neglect of the composition of output which renders the 'more growth versus less growth' controversy virtually meaningless. Economic growth is simply a measure of increased production of goods and services of any kind. Whether it is to be welcomed or deplored can only be decided by looking behind the aggregate and seeing what form it is taking. Only then are we in a position to relate growth to human welfare.

The present pattern of output in rich capitalist countries must be judged profoundly unsatisfactory. A very large proportion of it is made up of material trivia – the gadgetry of a consumer society. Some may take puritanical exception to the excesses of materialism. But for most people trivia can be fun. What *is* disturbing is the order of priorities implicit in an economic system which is highly geared to fulfilling second-order wants while failing to meet the needs of a large proportion of the population.

In Britain, for example, it is estimated that between 5–9 per cent of the population live on incomes below the supplementary benefit level, that is, in poverty according to the government's own definition. Taking a more generous view of what constitutes a tolerable standard of living (supplementary benefit level plus 40 per cent), the number falling below the poverty line is closer to seven and a half million.[1] For very many people, then, the market economy fails to fulfil their quite basic needs for food, warmth and shelter. This is because the pattern of output is a reflection of the distribution of income. Production for profit is naturally directed towards catering for the wants of those who can afford to satisfy them; there is no money to be made in alleviating the social distress of those short of purchasing power.

The basic solution to this imbalance in the composition of output therefore lies in redistributive measures outlined in previous chapters. But in lieu of these, if governments are *not* prepared to tackle the root problem of inequality, they must be prepared to treat the symptoms – modifying the pattern of output by charges and subsidies which ensure that needs are met before wants.

But suppose that incomes and wealth *were* more equally distributed. How far could we then leave matters to the market and expect a satisfactory composition of output to emerge? There are two reasons why, even in a more egalitarian framework, the market outcome would still be unacceptable. Firstly, the market cannot determine how resources should be divided between production of goods and services to be consumed privately and those which are consumed collectively. Secondly, the basis on which output decisions are taken in the market is narrowly commercial and neglects important costs and benefits which are external to individual enterprises. These two problems – of public or private goods and of 'externalities' – are, as will be seen, closely related.

We begin by asking whether, as a society, we want more public

1. A. B. Atkinson, *Poverty in Britain and the Reform of Social Security*, C.U.P., 1969.

goods or more private goods? As in the future we become materially still better off, do we want that affluence to take the form of more private consumption or do we want to enjoy it in collective consumption? Here once again is a real issue involving values rather than technical tinkering.

It is only sometimes a matter of public *versus* private. Education, for example, can be provided either privately through the market or collectively by the State – or by a combination of the two. But in some cases, such as national defence or law enforcement, we must either consume a service collectively or not have it all; it is simply not on for some taxpayers to opt out. And there is a third category of public consumption which is *complementary* to private consumption. Thus, for instance, more private ownership of cars means that more public provision of roads is needed.

The very phrase 'collective consumption' has rather unattractive connotations. It carries overtones of regimentation, drabness and bureaucratic inefficiency very different from the glitter and sparkle of brightly lit showrooms which we associate with private consumption. Nor is this simply a matter of words. It also seems to have substance in facts. Take, for example, the obvious case of private versus public transport. To own your own car gives you privacy, flexibility and the freedom of the roads. In contrast, public transport is often irregular, inflexible, overcrowded, slow and more expensive. But the basis of comparison is hardly a fair one. After all, *why* are urban bus services slow, infrequent and relatively expensive? Because of the congestion caused by private cars extravagant of road-space, because increased car ownership has reduced the demand for bus services and forced up their price. Given the resulting inadequacies of public transport there is every inducement for still more people to use their cars for the journey to work – to the consequent detriment of *both* other car users and those still travelling by bus. We are caught in a vicious circle. And the choice between private and public transport should be presented not in terms as they are now, but as alternative combinations of the two as they *could* be. If, for example, the car was banned from city centres, the quality and extent of public services which could then be provided would certainly be very different from what they currently offer.

Transport also provides an illustration of one of the more absurd, if not most serious, flaws in the present composition of output. The system fails to produce even those public goods necessary for the enjoyment of the private consumption to which the economy is primarily geared. An increase in the number of car owners requires an expansion of the road system. But road-building and town-planning have not kept pace – with the familiar results of urban snarl-ups, frustration, high accident rates and pollution. American experience suggests that the answer may not lie in bigger and better roads, because they merely increase car use still further and perpetuate the problem on a larger scale. We might therefore have to tackle the problem the other way round – by limiting car use to the capacity of the available roads. Striking the right balance is no easy matter. The important thing is that we should be able to see clearly what are the different packages of private and public consumption between which we have to choose. Generally at the present time these are not made clear.

The argument of this chapter will be that, in order to create a high quality of life and the necessary conditions for fuller enjoyment of private consumption, there is a strong case for increasing the proportion of resources going to the production of public goods and services. But in practice the economic system is heavily biased against increased collective consumption.

In the first place, in assessing our standard of living, how well off we are, most of us tend to concentrate on the amount of private consumption which we can manage to undertake. We generally fail to include as part of our total material welfare the benefits we derive from the range of public services which are provided – health, education, libraries, parks and so on. Awareness of the importance of these services is one of the reasons why American visitors to Britain sometimes argue with disbelieving natives that the U.K. standard of living is higher than their own.

A further bias against collective consumption arises from the fact that we do not all benefit equally from the provision of public services. We all help to pay for the building of inter-city motorways but the beneficiaries are the car-owners who use them. The childless still have to contribute towards the cost of schools. The healthy help to finance the treatment of the chronically sick. In other words, we do not always see any very direct link between what we pay and what we get back. Moreover, while considerable resources are poured into sectors like higher education, which, on ample evidence, is still largely enjoyed by children of middle-class parentage, other services which benefit much larger numbers are often relatively neglected. Replacement of antiquated school buildings in urban slums, the provision of parks, adventure playgrounds and low-cost housing lag behind partly because those who would benefit from them are less organized and vocal.

Then again there is the problem of financing public consumption. There is a deep-rooted prejudice against paying taxes. It is astonishing how many people remain convinced that taxes are largely frittered away in governmental extravagance and fail to connect them at all with the range of real benefits which they help to finance. This reluctance to see the 'burden of taxation' increased is, of course, fostered and reinforced by the whole ethos of the industrial system, which continually extols the virtues of more and more private consumption.

And yet the consequences of these biases in favour of private affluence as against more collective consumption are of a kind which perhaps the majority of people, when they think about it, find highly undesirable.

To begin with, a rule-of-thumb proposition could be put forward that the greater the proportion of output which goes to private rather than collective consumption the stronger will be the forces making for the perpetuation of inequality. Take, for example, the provision of education and health services. No one could deny that in these two areas enormous advances have been made since the war. But can we be satisfied that sufficiently rapid progress has been made in maintaining the quality of these services at a level which is appropriate to our growing material affluence? The National Health Service is constantly under fire – for its lack of comprehensiveness, its delays, its intrusions on personal privacy and dignity, on being over-pressured and consequently lacking in compassion. Vast areas of educational underprivilege continue to exist in the 1970s. The variations in the quality of schooling both within towns and between different parts of the country are often extreme. *One* of the reasons why these deficiencies have not been made good is the fact that education and medical care are also provided on a private, fee-paying basis by the market. Despite the extension of State education and health services, parallel systems of public schools and private provision for health have not only continued to exist but indeed seem to grow from strength to strength. Given a starting point of highly unequally distributed income and wealth, the result is predictable. The few who can afford to cater for their education and health needs by forking out of their own pockets tend to opt out of the State system. But it is these middle- and upper-income groups who generally have the strongest views about standards, who are most vociferous and capable of bringing pressure to bear on the relevant authorities to ensure that services of an acceptable quality are provided. Not only, then, is the provision of private education and medical care a direct expression of existing inequality. Not only does it perpetuate that inequality by giving the offspring of the privileged minority a better start in life. There is, on top of that, a detrimental feed-back for the State services – in the lack of push for improvement in their quality which would certainly come about if everyone, regardless of their social and economic position, had to use them.

The other chief arguments for increased collective consumption are those connected with the general quality of life and the need for public goods and services to be produced on a substantial scale if maximum enjoyment is to be derived from private consumption. Increasing lip-service is paid to the importance of enhancing the environment in which we live. Yet this will not happen through the workings of the market. Increasingly, as we grow richer, we shall require outlets for the constructive enjoyment of our leisure. Yet the fisherman today finds his sport ruined by polluted rivers, the family motorist sometimes reduced to picnicking in a litter-strewn layby. Cleaning up the mess already caused to the environment, providing the required range of leisure activities, including continued education, and generally creating conditions in which people find it pleasant to live will all require a shift to more collective consumption if the Galbraithian nightmare of 'private affluence, public squalor' is to be avoided.

If there is an imbalance in the present composition of output, then what – apart from the inequalities of income and wealth which have already been discussed – has brought it about? The principal culprit is the narrowness of the criterion which determines what and what is not produced for the market. The criterion is a simple one: those goods and services will be produced for which the price charged is sufficient to cover costs and yield an acceptable profit. All that shows in a private firm's accounts are the costs and returns as they appear to that company: these are the basis on which production decisions are taken. What is left out are the effects of these decisions on other elements in the economy. Costs and benefits can arise for the *rest* of the community as a result of the one firm's activities. The output pattern of the private sector is dictated by purely *commercial* considerations.

What has to be made clear is that 'commercial' is not to be equated with 'economic'. And, secondly, that there is no need for us to resign ourselves to the view that what is 'economic' is necessarily desirable, and that the 'non-economic' must always be rejected out of hand.

Because production is commercially viable – the revenue resulting from it exceeding the costs which firms have incurred – it does not always follow that it is economic. Nor do financial losses for a company necessarily indicate that it has been engaged in production which was uneconomic. Whether or not output is economic depends not just on if the companies concerned are doing well or badly, but on the net effect of their activities on the community as a whole. The difference between the economic as opposed to the commercial criterion is that it takes into account external or 'spill-over' effects.

Thus the factory that belches smoke into the surrounding neighbourhood or dumps its effluent into an adjoining river creates costs in the process. But they are not costs which will appear in its own balance sheet. They are costs which are borne by others – the housewife coping with the family washing, the bronchial patients in the doctor's waiting room, the local authority using the river as a source of drinking water and those who previously used the river for a variety of pleasurable activities. Similarly commercial airlines currently making profits would certainly not do so if they had to compensate those who bear the cost of aircraft noise in the districts surrounding major airports. Or take the matter of industrial location. The firm that sets up business in an area of already concentrated industrial activity does so because that is what is suggested by its estimates of private costs and yields. It is the community which carries the costs of straining resources and amenities which are already working near full capacity. If that firm could only be induced to move to a development area, not only would these additional social costs be avoided but positive benefits might result. The value of time wasted by every other road user does not show in the costing of a particular firm whose lorries add to an existing congestion problem; nor does the saving in unemployment benefit appear as part of the profit of a firm hiring labour in a development area. What makes sense for the economy as a whole may not seem so to the individual companies involved.

Private firms are concerned only with output which it *pays* them to produce. What it is economic to produce, on the other hand, can be decided only when wider spillover effects, both costs and benefits, are taken into account. But that should still not be the end of the matter – although it often is. Such is the sway which economics today has on our thinking that for a particular project to be labelled 'non-economic' is a clear indication that it should be consigned to the wastepaper basket. But are there no circumstances in which we think *non*-economic aspects important enough to outweigh purely economic considerations? Are we only interested in devoting resources to education, for example, if there are clear economic gains from doing so?

Ideally, then, the composition of output would be determined not on a commercial basis dictated by profit maximization but in such a way that spillover effects are fully taken into account and the production which takes place is that which maximizes the *social surplus* of benefits over costs. In principle this can be calculated by the use of cost-benefit analysis.

A well-known application of cost-benefit techniques is the study by C. D. Foster and M. Beesley of the economics of the Victoria Line extension to the London Underground railway system.[2] On a commercial basis, there seemed little prospect of the line paying its way. On the contrary, it was predicted that it would have an annual operating loss of about £2 million, with an additional loss of £1 million to the underground system as a whole as passengers took advantage of the shorter routes provided by the new line. However, Foster and Beesley tried to estimate the wider social benefits which would arise from the construction of the Victoria Line – for example, the time-savings both of those using the Victoria Line and those road-users now facing less congestion as a result of some surface-travellers now preferring to go by underground. They concluded that the economic as opposed to commercial return on the line might be of the order of 11 per cent.

Cost-benefit analysis offers the attractive possibility of establishing whether a project will be beneficial to society as a whole rather than just the individual enterprise involved in it. But cost-benefit analysis, like job evaluation, does not provide any objective, scientific answers. Its use for ranking projects in order of priority depends entirely on the values which are injected into analysis. For example, two of the external costs involved in the siting of a new international airport would certainly be the noise nuisance to local residents and passenger inconvenience caused by a particular situation. But quite apart from problems of measuring them, there is the further question of the relative *weights* which should be attached to the two costs. If, again, the benefits of a project exceed the costs but the benefits largely accrue to a minority of rich individuals while the costs are mostly borne by a majority of poorer people, should the project still be undertaken? We can either value costs and benefits at present

2. C. D. Foster and M. E. Beesley, 'Estimating the Social Benefit of Constructing an Underground Railway in London', *Journal of the Royal Statistical Society*, 1963.

market prices (which reflect the present distribution of income) and accept that a pound's worth of benefit or cost has the same value regardless of who gains or loses – which is an implicit acceptance of the principles underlying the status quo – or we can use 'shadow prices' reflecting a more optimal income distribution, and make deliberate judgements that certain classes of cost and benefit should count more heavily than others. In this case, we are talking about what *ought* to be. The virtue of cost-benefit analysis, once again like job evaluation, is that it forces decision-makers to take an explicit stand on relative social values.

Cost-benefit analysis is still in its infancy. Although it is in increasing use by government agencies in appraising projects, this is often done on a piecemeal basis. To show that a particular project will generate benefits in excess of costs does not necessarily mean that it should therefore be undertaken. Such a decision should be made only after the project has been compared with others, some of which may show a greater social surplus. But often cost-benefit analysis has been used to justify a particular investment without any attempt to put it in a ranking order with alternative schemes.

Use of cost-benefit analysis is particularly attractive for government departments, partly because it offers the possibility of measuring non-marketed services, and partly because the public sector accepts wider responsibilities than the purely commercial. But from the point of view of achieving a more acceptable composition of output, clearly the principle of taking into account social costs and benefits must be extended throughout the economy as a whole. If private enterprises operate on an exclusively commercial basis, serious divergencies between private and social gains and losses may emerge. But are firms still only profit-maximizers or have they already themselves begun to assume wider responsibilities? Should they be subject to 'social-efficiency audits' by a government body charged with ensuring that private and social objectives are kept broadly in line? The implications of achieving the real ends of economic policy as we have been setting them out – whether capitalism can be modified to bring them about or whether more fundamental changes are called for – are the subject of the following chapter.

18

Accountability, Planning and Involvement

If economic policy has confused ends with means, if economics itself is seen as an arid and callous discipline in which *people* don't really matter, if it is right to think that there is deep dissatisfaction amongst the mass of people in this country about the nature of our economic record, then there is also every reason to expect such discontent to become still stronger in the future. It can be avoided only if we face up to the real-world issues of fairness, of the extent to which people meaningfully fill their working lives and leisure and of securing a pattern of output which enhances rather than detracts from the quality of life. The course of failure in these respects has already been charted. As Thomas Balogh has written: 'it would be sad if our best hopes for the next twenty-five years would be limited to approaching today's American way of living. Something much more happy and satisfying is both needed, and possible.' But how? How can the economic system be humanized and given a purposeful social direction which it at present so patently lacks?

Some will argue, and they include both its advocates and critics, that the problems which we have been discussing are the inevitable by-products of capitalism. Supporters will say, for instance, that inequality is the price of economic dynamism and that only ruthless pursuit of profit regardless of other considerations will generate the capital accumulation on which future prosperity depends. Seen from the left, the implication is clear: it is capitalism itself which must be overthrown before we can create a humane and equitable society.

But there are also those who point to the enormous flexibility of the capitalist system and its ability to adjust. For them, capitalism is capable of self-reform and indeed is already involved in the process. Capitalism today, it is argued, is a very different animal from that portrayed by its opponents. No longer is it red in tooth and claw, narrowly striving after profit regardless of social consequences. Already it has begun to grow a human face. In the same way that it was able to accept the major increase in government economic intervention which Keynes showed was necessary if mass unemployment was to be eradicated, so from the 1970s it will emerge with new social responsibility and obligations.

The possibility that this could happen stems from the 'managerial revolution' which was discussed in Chapter 13 – the separation of ownership from control which means that firms, so long as they make satisfactory profits which keep their share-holders quiet, are free to pursue other goals. The technostructure of managers and technical experts who now effectively run large companies is, some say, essentially benevolent and socially aware. Not itself the recipient of the profits which result from the firm's activities, it *does* worry about the effects of its actions on employment, working conditions and social welfare – and its own public image. Far from being the bogeymen portrayed by left-wing critics, the new managers respond readily to the social pressures of their time with a concerned paternalism seen, for example, in the way in which some German firms cater for their workers' needs from the cradle to the grave.

No one claims that everything is already beautiful in the capitalist garden. Indeed one close observer, in a prize-winning contribution towards new thinking in management journalism, still sees the workings of capitalism as a reflection of an underlying violence. 'Businessmen are measured by the increase in profits, whatever the human cost ... The throwing of men onto the scrap-heap without any sense of responsibility for their future; the closure of factories without consultation; the making of vast profits from land speculation when hundreds of thousands are poorly housed ... all these may not involve physical blows but their consenquences, in the shape of the bitterness they create, are in a sense even more damaging.'[1] That there is still scope for im-provement is admitted, too, by a report by the company affairs

1. G. Turner, *Towards a New Philosophy for Industrial Society.*

committee of the Confederation of British Industry which suggests the need for a code of conduct to guide managers in 'making decisions with a social or ethical content; to provide them with a body of doctrine and to help raise the general standard of corporate behaviour'.[2]

Certainly Graham Turner is right in contending that 'nothing would have a greater impact in changing the tenor of a materialistic society than capitalists acting beyond their self-interest'. But when he goes on to ask 'Why should they not be the unexpected radicals in our midst? If businessmen accepted that challenge, they would be regarded not as soaks but saviours, not as defenders of an outworn creed but as forerunners and architects of a new society', there will be many sceptics and cynics who find his vision unconvincing and argue that the leopard has not and cannot change his spots. All that has happened is that firms have matured from a myopic quest for short-term profits to a realization that it is long-term profitability which really matters. It is in these terms, rather than in increased social responsibility, that any minor concessions to humanization must be seen. They are the price of ensuring the future of the system itself: 'survival' is a concept which constantly recurs in contemporary management literature.

Left-wing critics will argue that basically nothing has changed, and that behind the façade of giantism and technostructure it is still small groups of rich individuals who hold the reins and who remain very much concerned with maximizing profits. And there are businessmen themselves, like the director of a major multinational company, who persist in seeing as 'the primary objective of industry the maximization of profits after tax. If this simple point is overlooked and important social or political obligations are put ahead of the maximization of net profits, the result will be industrial and national stagnation ... Industrial leadership is without doubt a rat-race and must remain so. There is no hope for this country until we have a few more rats.'[3]

2. C. B. I., *A New Look at the Responsibilities of the British Public Company*, 1973.

3. Alun Davies, director of R T Z, quoted by Graham Searjeant, *Sunday Times*, 11 February, 1973.

On balance, it seems true that the private sector, whether because it sees its survival threatened or because it has positively embraced wider responsibilities, *is* becoming more socially sensitive. Take, for example, attitudes towards asset-stripping, the process of one company taking over another chiefly with the aim of closing down its unprofitable branches and selling them off without regard for the resulting redundancies. Once hailed as important contributors to industrial rationalization, firms specializing in this field have come to be viewed with growing distaste not only by the general public but also by the business community and even, in its downgrading of their share values, by the City. And perhaps, too, in a period when very large financial subsidies are available from governments, it is the firms which can closely knit their own aims with those of the authorities that are the most successful.

It is also possible to modify the effects of capitalism by altering the constraints within which it continues to pursue profit maximization or other self-interested goals. Changing the legal framework – by anti-pollutant standards or minimum of safety specifications – can certainly bring about a shift in the strategy by which a car manufacturer, for instance, achieves its commercial objectives. But organized resistance to such limitations on corporate freedom is generally considerable, as was illustrated by the notorious hounding of Ralph Nader by General Motors.

The Need for Planning

Our present economic system – if it is not to destroy the environment, dehumanize the work-force and engender gross inequalities and public impoverishment – requires a good deal more than minor piecemeal adjustment. Its nature excludes considerations of social costs and benefits, and, through inequalities of income and wealth, creates a structure of prices which makes it difficult for important externalities even to be properly evaluated. Matters like composition of output, distribution of income and content of employment are highly interrelated; the outcome of market forces in the present socio-economic framework is so different from that which most people would regard as equitable and acceptable that only a major shift in the balance between private and public power will bring about the results which most people say that they want.

These days, considerable lip-service is paid to notions of improved quality of life, a more caring society, a more congenial environment, more satisfying and rewarding working conditions. What is not always realized are the radical political implications of achieving these desiderata. They have not come about on their own; they have to be *planned* for.

The situation is analogous to the time when the Keynesian breakthrough first made it feasible to aim at full employment. Many of those who agreed that full employment was a laudable goal at the same time opposed government economic 'interference'. But what Keynes showed was that you can't have the one without the other: full employment can *only* be achieved if governments are prepared deliberately to manage the level of demand in the economy. Willing the 'end' of full employment meant willing the 'means' too – a major extension of State intervention in the form of demand management.

Similarly today, *if* we are concerned about the vast disparities of income and wealth which now exist and begin to question their basic justification, *if* the wider considerations of a social calculus are to be built into business accounting, then the implication is clear. In the absence of an improbable 'renaissance of moral and spiritual values' on which some pin their hopes, the only alternative of achieving a fairer and more humane society is for a further evolution to take place from a managed to a planned economy.

Planning in this country has rather a bad name. Many people instinctively recoil from the idea, because they associate it with totalitarianism and loss of individual freedom. They will also point to the wastes and bureaucratic absurdities of highly centralized planning as practised in the Soviet Union – the administrators at the top taking decisions which bear no relation to what consumers want, enterprises striving to fulfil output targets regardless of whether the output can be sold.

This is not the form of planning which is being advocated here. The nature and problems of the mature and affluent British economy as it is today are totally different from those of backward, underdeveloped economy of the post-revolution Soviet Union or, for that matter, those of the austere, war-wracked Britain of the late forties. And so also is the type of planning which is needed to deal with those problems.

But hasn't it already been tried? After all, there were two experiments in planning in the sixties – the Neddy blueprint for growth in 1962 and the subsequent National Plan for 1964–70. Both were shortlived and almost total failures. It is important to see why they foundered.

First of all, they failed because the planners got their sums wrong. Estimates had to be made about what would happen over the plan period to the various constituents of total demand and supply. This was no easy task, because on the demand side, for example, it involved forecasting the growth of private consumption, private investment, government spending and exports minus imports. Of these, investment and the foreign-trade balance are particularly difficult to predict in a mixed economy, because they depend on factors largely outside the government's control. In the event, the forecasts made in the two plans wildly missed the mark, and both plans came to an early demise chiefly because of unforeseen balance of payments crises.

Secondly, the planning experiments of the sixties did not provide for any major increase in the scope of government economic intervention. This was merely 'indicative' planning aimed at bringing together the various elements of the economy in order to demonstrate the extent of their common interest. It emphasized the degree of consensus rather than conflict which existed between the aims of industry, workers and government. Thus business, with its massive capital outlays, needed government to create an ordered future in which uncertainties could be minimized. Government, by bringing together all the parties concerned, could determine the feasibility of a future growth path and what it would mean to each of those involved. In such a process, workers would realize that in planned growth lay the prospect of regular increases in their *real* earnings rather than the illusory scramble for higher money wages in the inflationary jungle.

Permissive planning like this simply involves deciding what is possible, setting some targets, and then hoping that everyone concerned will do their bit to make the possible become reality. But supposing, as actually happened, that all were not equally convinced by the logic of the plan? Suppose that some did not play the part that had been assigned to them? Then, unless the authorities had the powers and used them to bring the recalcitrants into line, those who did follow the original blueprint would find that they had done so at their cost. But governments were not prepared to intervene positively along these lines. The plans lacked teeth.

And, finally, the attempts at planning in the sixties did not aim at a comprehensive range of objectives. Instead they focused almost exclusively on the question of how to increase Britain's rate of economic growth. Just how sensible it is to treat this index as a measure of anything significant is a matter which has already been discussed in earlier chapters. All in all, it is not surprising that 'the passage from panacea through bitter experience to music-hall joke which had been planning's fate in the first decade after the Second World War was repeated fifteen years later'.[4]

As with incomes policy, the repeated failures of planning in the past strengthen the prejudice against its reintroduction again. But if planning is defined as systematic intervention by the authorities to bring about changes in the economy in accordance with an overall strategy, it is difficult to see how the real issues with which we have been concerned *can* be dealt with without recourse to planning. The question is not whether or not to plan but what scope and form planning should have. Is there an alternative to highly centralized direction of the economy along the Soviet lines and the ineffectual variety of weakly permissive planning?

There is such an alternative if only there were the political will to grasp the nettle of inequality. Within a more egalitarian framework many of the objections to the way of the market are removed. If consumers had more or less equal 'voting power',

4. R. Opie, 'Economic Planning and Growth', in W. Beckerman (ed.), *The Labour Government's Economic Record 1964–70*, p. 177.

the 'planning versus market' dichotomy could be transformed into a recognition that a good deal of planning could take place *through* the market. Particularly in an affluent economy where complex decisions have to be taken about which particular combination of consumer goods should be produced, the market mechanism has much to commend it as a method of allocating resources. Many of the defects of the market system in practice are due to the 'imperfections' which mar it. Socialize the framework in which market forces work and they can be left to determine a large proportion of productive decisions.

There are certainly substantial areas in which planning involves more direct intervention: the allocation of resources between private and public consumption, between consumption and investment and between goods produced for the home market and those for export could still not safely be left to the market to determine even if the economy had a more egalitarian basis. Then, too, there is the question of how the behaviour of firms could be modified so that they take into account social rather than private gains and losses.

That these are all areas which require control from above will confirm the suspicions of those who believe that planning involves curtailment of present individual and corporate freedom. They are right. But what must be remembered is that 'freedom' within the present system is for the few. Like income and wealth, it is highly unequally distributed. Although planning would mean more rigid overall control of the economy by the State at the expense of a reduction in the liberty of individuals and firms to take decisions on a private rather than a social basis, a *quid pro quo* could be an extension of involvement for the mass of people in the determination of their everyday economic lives.

Even the establishment of a 'fairer' society will not resolve the deep-rooted alienation of labour from capital and the social and economic tensions and conflicts which result from it. As Dr Ota Sik has put it: 'Wage earners are interested only in increasing their wages. They have no direct interest in capital, the growth of capital, the use of profits or decisions on investments.'[5] And

5. O. Sik, *The Times*, 4 October 1972.

this is as true in those communist countries where capital has been taken over by the State as it is in the industrial economies of the West. It holds good as much in our own nationalized industries as it does in the private sector.

'Only where man has an immediate economic interest in the future development of an enterprise, in investment, in the effectivity of new capital equipment and so on, will he gradually begin to be master of his own conditions of production.'[6] This surely is the direction in which we shall have to move in coming decades – not merely because it is perhaps the only way in which we can come to grips with our present inflationary troubles, but also because for individuals to have a say in controlling their own economic destinies is a worthwhile objective in itself.

What is called for is not simply profit-sharing, but *capital*-sharing, so that ultimately those engaged in an enterprise come to own it collectively. What is needed is not the occasional worker-director on the board of a company, but the dispersion of power throughout the firm as a whole. Such a programme of radical reform would certainly arouse violent opposition from those powerful and deeply entrenched interests who are the major beneficiaries of our present system, and much could be written about the political and practical mechanics of bringing about such fundamental changes. But first it is important to debate the principle itself; here again, as with many of the other 'big' questions we have touched upon, what is disturbing is that in Britain today there is so little open public discussion even about whether it is *right* that democracy should stop at the polling-booth and that the economy should be governed according to a quite different set of values.

6. ibid.

19

Some International Constraints

There is a substantial ground-swell of dissatisfaction with the way in which the economy works and a questioning, sometimes from unexpected quarters, of the accepted economic 'goals' of post-war economic policy. But the criticism is fragmented. Different groups concentrate on particular shortcomings of the economic system: their concern is with pollution or unfairness, conservation, social accountability or lack of participation. Seen as a whole, the implications of dealing with these various aspects of the problem in a systematic manner turn out to be far more radical than is sometimes thought.

That is the argument so far – and it has been cast in an insular mould. But in fact Britain is, and always will be, deeply enmeshed in the international economy. The question to which we must now turn is therefore whether the growing internationalism of recent years helps or hinders the solution of what have been proposed as Britain's 'real' economic problems? What, in particular, will be the effect on these issues of British membership of an enlarged European Economic Community?

The first point to be cleared up is that, as things stand at the moment, it is certainly not the case that a radical and economically enlightened Britain has teamed up with a group of reactionary or relatively conservative laggards. On the contrary, in many areas of social and economic policy, it is Britain which has been least adventurous in taking new initiatives. Take, for instance, the matter of employee involvement. In Britain it is possible to find examples of profit-sharing, such as the John Lewis Partnership, and even of capital-sharing, as in I.C.I. and the very remarkable instance of the Scott Bader company, in which the private proprietors virtually handed ownership over to their employees. But these are isolated cases. In France, on the other hand, since 1968 *all* firms with more than a hundred employees have had to implement profit-sharing schemes. The German policy of *Mitbestimmung* ensures that in large firms there are worker-directors on the boards. And in Denmark the government is preparing to introduce legislation which would mean that employees would eventually control any company with more than fifty on its pay roll. Similarly, in the fields of incomes policy, planning and public enterprise, there are many continental examples of experiments way ahead of anything that has so far been attempted in this country.

But suppose that at some stage Britain did take the lead in bringing about a fundamental redistribution of income and wealth, a market system based on a social calculus within an overall planning strategy, a shift from private to public consumption and widespread participation of employees in determining their working conditions. How would such a system fare in the context of an open international economy?

Assuming that other countries meanwhile continue to pursue conventional policies and goals, then 'the open frontiers of the Community, the agreements to abstain from impeding the movement of people, goods and money, would greatly complicate the political problem. The danger would be that, for example, an exceptionally heavy tax to discriminate sharply against company profits or the ownership of capital would induce the people who felt that they were being badly treated to move their resources to other, more friendly parts of the Community. A single national government on its own would find it very hard to stand up against this.'[1]

The picture painted here is one in which Britain would suffer, in the first place, a brain drain – as managers, professional people and skilled workers took the opportunity to earn more in other countries not pursuing egalitarian policies. Capital, too, would flee to more congenial climes and the inflow of new foreign investment would dry up. Britain might as a consequence become relatively poorer – and would this not cause growing resentment,

1. A. Shonfield, 'Journey to an Unknown Destination', The Reith Lectures, *The Listener*, 9 November 1972.

as the British people saw their standards of living slip further and further behind those in neighbouring economies?

But there are also grounds for taking a rather more optimistic view of the outcome. Firstly, the notion that large numbers would pack their bags and go is to some extent question-begging. The basic changes in our socio-economic system which we have been considering would come about only *if* there was a general acceptance that they would lead to a society which was altogether more attractive than the present one. What has been proposed is a much more than simply opting out of a competitive growth race. It involves a very positive 'opting in' to a quite different and more purposeful scale of economic and social priorities. Even today it is interesting how many British citizens, lured abroad by the prospects of higher earnings, subsequently return, having in the meantime recognized that the qualitative aspects of a society sometimes count more than material affluence.

In any case, the basic changes which we have been discussing are not directed against materialism as such. The argument has not been that economic growth is wrong, but that we should be concerned with the nature of that growth. How much more we should try to increase our material affluence is a question which remains open for choice. The important thing is that the choice is made deliberately rather than that we continue to be swept along in the blind momentum of an international rat-race. It is very possible that a society which is not rent by industrial conflict and a deep sense of underlying unfairness may even prove to be *more* economically efficient, and there is no particular reason to assume that such a Britain would become markedly less competitive in international markets.

However, the prospect of Britain going it alone in establishing a new social and economic order seems extraordinarily unlikely. At the moment, as has been pointed out, Britain if anything lags behind in seeking fundamental answers to fundamental questions. And if and when progress is made in that direction it is much more probable that changes will be brought about roughly in parallel between countries responding to very similar pressures and tensions.

The basic ethos and the structure of the E.E.C. do not at first sight, suggest it as a very promising launching-pad for ideas of radical change. To begin with, at least in the way in which it has been presented, it is a bloc even more single-mindedly oriented towards the quest for faster economic growth than we are. Indeed the principal argument put forward in favour of British entry into Europe was that, somehow, association with high-growth performers would make us better at it too. One level of opposition was to question how or whether this would happen. Yet another was to ask if it would be desirable if it did.

Moreover, critics will point to the extent to which an essentially market philosophy is built into the Treaty of Rome – with its emphasis on competition and liberalization of trade. But market forces, we have been arguing, unless they are working within a planned and equitable framework, are bound to lead to serious imbalances, injustices and anomalies.

Then again, some of the political aspects of the Community are *prima facie* disturbing. In Britain, the growing size of the enterprises for which they work and the remoteness of the government machinery which attempts to control them leaves ordinary people with a sense of inadequacy, a feeling of working towards goals which are largely irrelevant to them and being unable to do anything about it. The result can be seen in the extent to which people are increasingly taking power into their own hands, short-circuiting traditional parliamentary methods of achieving their aims, and resorting to direct action, whether it be in the form of industrial confrontation or local pressure groups agitating against attempts to impose neighbourhood detriments like a new airport or motorway. It is this which leads to anxious speculation that the country is increasingly becoming 'ungovernable'. But if Whitehall and Westminster seem far away, how much more remote is the way in which matters will be decided in a wider Europe? 'It is a fact that the Community has developed a network of "official channels" which the man in the street can make nothing of. He knows that important decisions – which affect his own immediate affairs – are being taken at the European level, but he does not know exactly who takes them, or who has to carry them out, or how. The Commission proposes, the European Parliament gives opinions, the Council decides – and without more ado, the individual citizen is committed.'[2]

That was the view of Dr Sicco Mansholt, President of the European Commission – strangely enough, the very body whose bureaucratic unaccountability has been the major target of those who allege that the Community is essentially undemocratic. Even stranger was the occasion on which he expressed that view – a dinner held at Hampton Court Palace on 2 January 1973 to celebrate Britain's entry into Europe. What might have been expected in the circumstances was a fanfare trumpeting of the Community's achievements. What in fact the outgoing President of the Commission had to say not only made nonsense of many of the arguments which the British Government had been putting forward as the case for Britain joining Europe; it was also extremely relevant to the argument of this book.

The European Community, said Mansholt, 'had failed to fire most people's imagination. I do not think I am going too far when I say that what we have done so far has not come up to the European public's expectations. People cannot feel that what we have done is anything new; Europe has still not given a new dimension to life.' Moreover, he went on to argue that 'the progress of integration has led to major social stresses. The disparities in standards of living between different areas of the Community have become more marked rather than less. For the great mass of the population there has been no broad improvement in conditions generally. Dissatisfaction is indeed widespread . . .' And he was quite able to understand both that great numbers of Norwegians, for example, 'simply could not see the point of what we are doing' and the British tendency to 'think of the Europe of Multinational Corporations rather than the Europe of the Peoples'.

Here, in other words, is confirmation of the worst suspicions of the anti-Marketeers – that free trade and competition, between unequals, will be further disequalizing, that increases in gross national product do not automatically guarantee even improved standards of living, let alone enhance the quality of life. But Mansholt nonetheless retains a vision of what Europe

2. *The Times*, 3 January 1973.

could become: 'a rigorously planned economy' aimed at eliminating pollution and conserving resources, a society in which 'If gross national product is no longer the goal . . . then attitudes to social position and to work will change'.[3]

One aspect of the growing internationalism of the post-war years which most clearly represents a threat to the ability of any single nation to determine its own economic destiny is the development in recent decades of those giant industrial companies which now bestraddle the world. Monsters like General Motors, most of the oil companies, General Electric, I.B.M. and Unilever have grown to a size which seriously endangers national sovereignty.

Such companies, because their operations no longer coincide with national boundaries, are in a position where they can to a large degree circumvent national attempts to regulate them. For example, being free to locate anywhere they choose, they will concentrate their operations in areas which are attractive because of cheap labour supply, where trade unions are not highly organized, where governments offer tax concessions and can guarantee political stability albeit through an oppressive régime. They can play one government off against another in deciding where to site new plants and avoid situations where they are expected to bear social costs of, for example, pollution or redundancy. They can create imbalances in an economy by using only its manual work-force while importing managerial personnel from outside and concentrating their research activities in another country.

Given the scale of the internal transactions between their various subsidiaries, the multinationals are in a position to limit their tax burden and determine where it should be paid. This they can do though the technique of 'transfer pricing' – setting artificially low or high prices on parts and components exchanged between different branches of the company. In this way they can show low profits in those countries with high tax rates, and declare higher profits only where taxation is light. Rio Tinto

3. *Sunday Times*, 25 June 1972.

Zinc, for instance, pays only 2 per cent of its total tax bill in Britain. British Petroleum pays none at all.[4]

Their scale of internal finance and access to international sources make the multinationals relatively impervious to national monetary policies. Moreover, not only are they also able to avoid exchange control restrictions on the outflow of capital by, once again, internalizing their transactions; they can also contribute to exchange rate instability by shifting vast sums from country to country in anticipation of devaluations and revaluations. In the process, they are, of course, making such adjustments more likely. One observer in fact suggests that the amount of transactions which multinationals are now carrying out across national boundaries 'has risen so much that they have enough resources practically to bring about a currency devaluation once they have made up their minds that this is about to happen'.[5]

Multinationals can also frustrate the attempts of national governments to right their balance of payments. A subsidiary in one country may be discouraged from producing components which therefore have to be imported from another overseas branch. Market sharing may take place between a handful of giant rivals anxious to avoid competition with each other. Thus when, for example, the British government is seeking to increase exports to the United States, the fact that there is no response from Company X may be because it has an agreement with Company Y to concentrate on the British market and leave America to Company Y.

As Wayland Kennet has concluded: 'There has been an uncovenanted passage of sovereignty from national governments to international corporation ... sovereignty is seeping away downwards into the invisible tuber system of politically irresponsible capital.'[6] It may well be that 'the great world monopolies ... have no ambitions to govern',[7] but they are certainly very concerned about who does govern and according to what rules – as was

4. Wayland Kennet, Larry Whitty, Stuart Holland, *Sovereignty and Multi-National Companies*, Fabian Tract 409, 1971, p. 1.

5. Louis Turner, *Politics and the Multi-National Company*, Fabian Research Series 279.

1. Kennet, op. cit.   2. Bowen, op. cit., p. 21.

shown by the scandalous attempts of I.T.T. to use the machinery of the C.I.A. to prevent the emergence of a communist régime in Chile.

The ability of a giant international firm to challenge an individual government is well illustrated by the affair of Hoffman-La Roche, the Swiss-based drugs manufacturing group. Acting in April 1973 on the basis of a Monopolies Commission report, the British government ordered large cuts in the price paid by the National Health Service for two tranquillizers, Librium and Valium, produced by the group – and also demanded repayment of more than £2 million of excess profits made in the past. Not only did Hoffman-La Roche refuse to make any such repayment. They also proposed retaliation at any effort to reduce their prices.

Senior directors of the group emphasized that they did not want to adopt a threatening posture towards the British Government, but the economics of the situation might demand harsh measures. These could include: 1. Blocking the export, particularly to Commonwealth or former Commonwealth countries, of 'specialist' products, made or finished in the United Kingdom – including Librium and Valium. 2. Transferring the manufacturing facilities for active ingredients used in pharmaceuticals other than Librium and Valium out of the United Kingdom. 3. Making a drastic revision of research investment plans, probably involving the siting of new research facilities outside Britain.[8]

If an attempt to curb excessive prices and profits can evoke a challenge as open and formidable as this from a single firm, some idea can be formed of how much more devastating would be the concerted response of multinationals as a whole to moves by an individual government in the direction of radical economic and social reform. It is difficult to avoid the conclusion that here *is* a major constraint on the ability of any single major industrial economy to introduce a programme of fundamental change.

The traditional solution of nationalization does not work in this case because generally a subsidiary of a multinational is heavily dependent on inputs from and sales to branches of the company in other countries. What therefore would be taken over would often be assets virtually useless in themselves. And so far

8. Report in *The Times*, 28 April 1973.

'no concept has emerged that can reconcile global organization and social ownership'.[9]

If the challenge of the multinationals is to be met, then it can only be through the development of countervailing power. The trade unions have already begun to move in this direction by proposing international collective bargaining with the multi-nationals to ensure that the interests of workers in one country are not played off against those in another. But ultimately the remedy must lie in joint action by governments of a like mind – or the build-up of political units more powerful than present nation states.

Given the present international power structure it therefore seems probable that the goals which we have been discussing in previous chapters could be fully attainable only in a wider context than Britain alone. Whether we like it or not, we are left with the Mansholt vision of a humane and purposeful Europe.

9. Louis Turner, op. cit., p. 26.

20

The Poorest of the Poor

The inequities and distortions which exist within affluent economies are totally dwarfed by the division of the world into rich and poor nations. It is in this broad international setting that questions of 'what most people regard as urgent and menacing' are of the most profound importance. It is at this level that the issues which we have been discussing are posed with a stark and disturbing clarity. The continued existence of poverty and world inequality on their present scale represent *the* most pressing economic problem of our times. Incredibly, it is a matter to which mainstream economics has devoted relatively little attention.

The present economic system has resulted in the evolution of a 'development gap' of gigantic proportions, a gap which year by year is widening rather than narrowing. While a small group of nations wrestle with the problems of gross affluence, the majority of the world's population live in poverty and deprivation almost unimaginable for those in rich countries. How has this absurd and morally intolerable situation come about?

World inequality stems from basically the same causes as those defects of our own economy which have been the subject so far. They are the outcome of ostensibly 'fair' and 'free' market forces working within a framework which is itself imperfect and inequitable. Unregulated, the code of the market is little more than the law of the jungle in which benefits accrue only to those strong enough to seize them – whatever the initial source of their strength. The present development gap is the product of a century and a half of the disequalizing operation of such market forces.

In its broadest terms, the blame can be laid at the door of

'free trade' – the doctrine that it is best for nations, like individuals, to specialize according to their particular advantages and to exchange their surpluses without impediment from import duties, quotas and other 'barriers' to the free movement of goods in the international market. The original proponents of the free-trade theory argued that this maximizing of international trade was the way to secure the greatest *world* welfare – and that in the process all would benefit. Whether an economy was advanced or backward, industrial or heavily dependent on agriculture, rich or poor – *all* the partners in the free-trade enterprise would gain. It would pay them all to open their doors to the freest interchange.

Take, for example, an extreme case of two countries, one of which could produce all goods more efficiently than the other. Surely, in this case at least, there is nothing for either of them in the notion of specialization and trade? On the contrary, argued the free traders. The more efficient should still specialize in output where its advantage over the other is the greatest. If country X produces both industrial and primary goods more cheaply than country Y, but its advantage is most marked in industrial goods, then it will pay it to concentrate on industrial production, increase output accordingly – and in the process secure its primary products more cheaply through exports than it could by producing them itself. The less efficient Y, meanwhile, will obviously have benefited through being able to import cheaper industrial goods.

What could be fairer? Certainly, David Ricardo and the others who helped to give birth to the free-trade doctrine in the nineteenth century saw it as a way, not only of increasing the size of the world economic cake, but also ensuring that all who participated in its baking got a bigger slice. How then can it now be denigrated as an engine for perpetuating and widening international economic inequalities?

First of all, the outcome of free trade very much depends on the initial starting-point of the parties concerned. And by the beginning of the nineteenth century, an initial inequality had already emerged. A handful of European economies and economies originally peopled from Europe had begun a breakthrough to modern industrial growth. Moreover, they had established a political dominance over much of the rest of the world which enabled them to impose on it a trade pattern of their own choosing. It was they who would concentrate on manufactured goods. Others would specialize in the production of raw materials. To ensure that this was so, the metropolitan powers when necessary destroyed industries in the subordinate territories, as in the classic case of Indian textiles, or tried to prevent their emergence (though unsuccessfully in the case of the American colonies).

Trade was therefore between unequals. The Ricardian claim that all would gain *might* still be true. But how would the gains be divided between those taking part in international trade? Everything suggests that a state of 'free' competition between unequals can be exploited more successfully by the stronger partner. Although both may gain, it will be the stronger which gains most. The rich may get richer and the poor may get richer, but the rich get richer at a faster rate. And that is what has happened. The classical doctrine, adopting a world view, neglected the question of how the undoubted benefits of international trade would be shared out. This is typical of traditional economic theory: to try to separate matters of economic efficiency (which can be discussed in objective terms) from those of distribution (which involve making value judgements). But obviously, from the point of view of the poorer nations, distribution is the vital issue. Their concern is not so much with the size of the world cake as with how big a slice of it comes their way. It may well be the case that by having only limited trade they could do a great deal better.

Moreover, the division of labour which was established historically between rich and poor countries was a deeply unfair one. It may at first sight seem obviously sensible that countries should specialize along complementary lines. Manufacturers need raw materials, foodstuffs and primary producing countries need manufactures. But the demand and supply conditions for manufactures and primary products are very different. As world incomes grow, it may be true that demand for both industrial and primary products increases. But as we get richer we spend a smaller proportion of our incomes on foodstuffs. The growth in world demand will be much greater for industrial products. And on the supply side, not only are the opportunities for applying technical change in mass production much greater in manufacturing industry than in agriculture; industrial countries also have the ability to produce synthetic substitutes for natural raw materials.

It may well be the case that some of the countries currently specializing in primary production would have had a comparative advantage in manufactures had they been allowed to develop in that direction. It may still be the case that *potential* comparative advantage suggests a quite different pattern of output from the present one. But, at least in a free-trade situation, it is impossible for poor countries ever to get their infant industries off the ground in face of competition from established producers already enjoying the economies of scale. What is more, the present industrial nations not only have the advantage *now*; they are also in the position, by spending more on research and development into new products and processes, cumulatively to widen that lead over the years.

It is no wonder that underdeveloped countries label an organization like G.A.T.T. (General Agreement on Tariffs and Trade) as essentially a 'rich man's club'. G.A.T.T. has worked throughout the post-war period for liberalization of trade on the principle of reciprocity: that countries should match each others' cuts in trade restrictions and extend these concessions to all other members of the international trading community. But if the development gap is ever to be reduced, this will not do at all for the developing countries. What *they* need is the right to protect themselves against competition from the more advanced economies, while at the same time enjoying free access to the markets of the rich. Indeed what is called for is not merely equal terms of exchange but positive discrimination in favour of the poorer nations.

Free-trade theory, which purported to be objective economics of universal applicability, is nothing of the sort. It was the product of thinking in white, nineteenth-century, relatively advanced capitalist economies. Although the inventors of the doctrine may not have realized it, it was heavily biased in favour of the rich industrial nations. And it continues to be so today.

Similar effects follow from other aspects of international economic liberalization. For example, the policy-makers lay much stress on the importance of allowing free movement of capital, labour and technical knowledge between economies. Theory again suggests that such mobility will be generally beneficial. But in practice it is once more a case of the poor being the relative losers from such transfers.

For, in fact, perfect mobility would often lead to perverse movements – from poor economies to rich ones. Many wealth-holders in underdeveloped economies would like nothing better than to switch their capital to safer and more profitable use in rich countries – and they often succeed in illicitly doing so. Labour, when immigration laws allow it, moves in the same direction. But unfortunately, it is generally that skilled labour – doctors, nurses and graduates – which the poor countries can least afford to lose. The same mechanism of cumulative causation which we have already seen working to create personal and regional inequalities within a country also perpetuates and widens international disparities.

Even when capital and technical knowledge *are* transferred from advanced to underdeveloped economies, it is generally into narrow sectors. The modern, industrial urban areas are those which are most attractive to both private foreign investment and to official aid. The result is that foreign capital and technology, instead of spreading economic development, more often accentuate the basically *dualistic* nature of underdeveloped economies. Output from the modern sector kills off traditional industries. But, being based on the economics of the rich West, it is a technology which uses a lot of capital and economizes on labour – which is what poor economies happen to have in embarrassing abundance. It therefore adds to the massive unemployment which is already the most desperate of the problems of the Third World and which is bound to become still worse – the product, not just of population explosion but also of misguided educational and wage policies which have led to a futile and fatal drift from the rural sector. Moreover, not only is modern technology rather inefficient, because it is alien and inappropriate for those at a different stage of development; foreign investment is also essentially homeward-looking, involving an unwanted outflow of profits, interest and dividends.

Altogether, then, the cards are heavily stacked against the poorer two-thirds of the world. And in their policies on trade, aid and investment the rich few show little inclination to bring about any change in this fundamentally unjust state of affairs.

The case of underdeveloped countries highlights not only the issue of inequality, but also the absurdity of using increases in gross national product as a measure of economic progress. Judged by this dubious criterion, the record of the Third World is distinctly impressive. Historically unprecedented growth rates, averaging 4 per cent in the sixties, for example, might suggest that underdeveloped economies have finally 'taken off'. But quite apart from the fact that the growth performance of the rich economies was even better during these years, and that a good deal of increased output in poor countries was swallowed up by rapidly increasing population, the nonsense of equating growth with progress is even more patently obvious in the case of underdeveloped economies than it is in the affluent West.

For once we look behind the growth rates, what do we find in a typical underdeveloped country? In the first place, it will be suffering from unemployment and underemployment on a scale which, although difficult to measure precisely because of the inadequacy of statistics, far exceeds the worst excesses of the 1930s slump in the advanced industrial economies. It differs from unemployment in the rich countries in being chronic. These are not people who had jobs and have lost them. Most of them may never have had a job at all. Such unemployment cannot be solved by Keynesian techniques of pumping in more demand – which worked in the rich countries because capital as well as labour was lying idle. In the poor world, there is no spare capital to be drawn into production. The problem of unemployment, already of alarming proportions, is persistently deteriorating as high rates of population increase throw millions of young people each year onto a labour market which, with present policies and techniques, cannot conceivably absorb them.

Moreover, if income and wealth are very unequally distributed in rich countries, such disparities are even more marked in the underdeveloped world. Widening inequalities abound not just between individuals but also between regions and between town and countryside, with a relatively prosperous urban modernity superimposed on an impoverished traditional rural sector. It is not surprising that the resulting pattern of output is one which can satisfy the demands of the few for air conditioners, motor cars and refrigerators while leaving millions to suffer from serious malnutrition.

Concentrating on the growth index conceals all these vital considerations. Development means more than growth. However difficult to measure, it must have a qualitative as well as a quantitative dimension. Achieving development is not simply a matter of manipulating certain key economic variables within a given socio-economic context. It involves changing the context itself and basically transforming attitudes and institutions. Above all, it requires the political will to overcome the many anti-developmental interests which exist both inside and outside poor countries.

In the preceding chapter we looked at some of the international constraints on bringing about radical changes in an economy such as our own. How free are present underdeveloped countries to exercise a conscious option about the type of development they follow? Are they doomed to a pursuit of economic growth regardless of its consequences?

Given present levels of poverty in the Third World, the question of whether they should try to achieve material or nonmaterial ends is an unreal one. For the time being they simply have to concern themselves with increasing output. The immediate issue is how that should be done. Only at a later stage does the matter of how far they go along the road of material advancement become relevant.

Many of them, however, already seem set on what looks like the typical growth pattern pioneered by the early nineteenth-century developers. Broadly, it can be characterized as a sacrificial process in which jam tomorrow can be won only at the price of regrettable but inevitable hardship today. Inequality and unbalanced development are seen as the necessary cost of achieving the breakthrough to higher standards of living for all at a later state. It is a harsh and painful type of development based on essentially unplanned private enterprise. But it may be working in cases like Hong Kong, Formosa, South Korea. These countries have suffered a considerable loss of national identity in the process. But, nonetheless, basic changes have been brought about, with the mass of people involved in the dynamics of change – although they may not all be beneficaries.

But for many other countries, their close involvement with the western world through trade, investment and aid has succeeded only in creating pockets of capitalist activity without disturbing the underlying social fabric. The idea that the modern enclave will ultimately absorb the traditional sector of the economy seems far less plausible than the view that they will turn out to be 'mutually poisoning'. What is worrying about this group is that they are economies in which all the hardships of capitalist development are imposed without any guarantee that its ultimate fruits will be realized. What is also disturbing is the fact that few of them appear to have consciously opted for this particular type of development. In many ways they ostensibly try to resist it – with declarations of socialist values often built into their very constitutions and considerable lip-service paid to the ideal of planning. But, in practice, their enmeshment with western markets, western ideas and technology means that this is no more than an ideological façade.

Only a few have from the outset determined that their course of development should be a radically different one. China, Burma and Tanzania provide examples of the very diverse alternatives which are open. China is probably big enough to get away with it on its own. Burma, because of its anti-materialist emphasis, can also perhaps afford isolationism. But it is the Tanzanias of the world which are in real difficulty. Aiming from the start at an egalitarian rural development based on an appropriate technology, Tanzania's smallness and desperate poverty make it hard for it to remain independent of the outside world. But it is also difficult for it to secure the help it needs on terms which will not distort the philosophy of its development.

The chasm which separates the rich countries from the poor is merely a magnification of the processes at work within our own economy. The mechanisms which create such basic economic injustices are the same. And perhaps we shall only be able to contribute towards solving the problem of international inequality when we have put our own house in order. The discrepancy between the ideals to which we subscribe domestically and the policies which we pursue externally would then become even more painfully apparent than they are now.

Index

MORE ABOUT PENGUINS
AND PELICANS

A DICTIONARY OF ECONOMICS
Graham Bannock, R. E. Baxter and Roy Rees

A Penguin Dictionary of Economics is addressed to both the
student and the general reader who wants to be able to follow
economic discussions in the press and elsewhere, or whose daily
work demands some familiarity with economic terms. It aims to
provide a comprehensive companion to support other reading in a
discipline which employs remarkably similar terminology in Britain
and the United States.

A HANDBOOK OF MANAGEMENT
Edited by Thomas Kempner

A Handbook of Management provides an invaluable alphabetical
guide to the main ideas and techniques connected with the handling
of men, money, machines and markets. Over 1000 cross-referenced
entries define and clearly explain the salient facts (within the context
of industry and commerce) about all aspects of business. This store
of up-to-date information will certainly appeal to active managers,
teachers, and students of business, but the handbook is also likely to
attract anybody who wants to understand better the business
columns in the press.

A DICTIONARY OF COMMERCE
Michael Greener

Do you know the rule of Estoppel? The terms a kite, a kangaroo, a
lame duck? The difference between a feme sole and a feme covert?
All about Fire Insurance, the G.P.O., and British Rail?

This Penguin Reference Book, specially designed to resolve the
increasing complexity of business life for the man-in-the-street,
answers the above and many more queries on all aspects of commerce.
For, *Ignorantia juris haud excusat* – Ignorance of the law is no
excuse! and this ready-to-use handbook gives the literal meaning,
the usage and the limitations of those commercial terms which interest
the layman as businessman, taxpayer, and investor.

INFLATION

A Guide to the Crisis in Economics

J. A. Trevithick

Inflation, accompanied by economic disarray and popular despair, constitutes a major challenge to the credibility of economic science. Explanations and panaceas are vaunted, as various as they are incomprehensible, but the currency nonetheless continues to lose value.

Now, in this Pelican Original, Dr Trevithick opens up the discussion to include everyone, blasting away the jargon with well-informed clarity. The characters in the drama include Milton Friedman, Keynes, Hayek and the Cambridge Economic Policy Group, while the plot encompasses the Phillips Curve, Trade Union Power, 'Helicopter Money', floating currencies, incomes policy and indexation.

Theories differ – and not along the traditional political lines of left or right – but Dr Trevithick shows that it *is* possible to control inflation, and that no one measure is enough. A combination of treatments is required, based on a full understanding of the disease.